Virginia
Trout
Streams

Virginia
Trout
Streams

A GUIDE TO
FISHING THE
BLUE RIDGE
WATERSHED

By Harry Slone

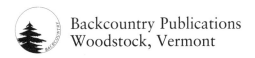

Backcountry Publications
Woodstock, Vermont

An Invitation to the Reader

With time, access points may change, and road numbers, signs, and land-marks referred to in this book may be altered. If you find that such changes have occurred near the streams described in this book, please let the author and publisher know, so that corrections may be made in future editions. Other comments and suggestions are also welcome. Address all correspondence to:

Fishing Editor
Backcountry Publications
P.O. Box 175
Woodstock, Vermont 05091

Library of Congress Cataloging-in-Publication Data
Slone, Harry, 1929–
    Virginia trout streams: a guide to fishing the Blue Ridge
  Watershed / Harry Slone
        p.   cm.
    Includes index.
    ISBN 0-88150-207-3
    1. Trout fishing—Virginia.   I. Title.
  SH688.U6S56 1991
  799. 1'755—dc20   91-25995
                                            CIP

10 9 8 7 6 5 4 3 2 1

Published by Backcountry Publications
A division of The Countryman Press, Inc.
Woodstock, Vermont 05091

Cover design by Donna Wohlfarth
Text design by Rachel K. Mahler
Maps by Richard Widhu © 1991
Cover photograph courtesy Virginia Division of Tourism
Photograph on page 41 by Kenneth E. Norton; on pages 77 and 126 by Harry Steeves; on pages 104 and 139 by Steve Hiner; all other photographs by the author.

Printed in the United States of America

DEDICATION

This book is for Mary Ann, who was dedicated to the joy of fly-fishing Virginia's mountain streams. Throughout her gentle lifetime she never took the life of even a single trout.

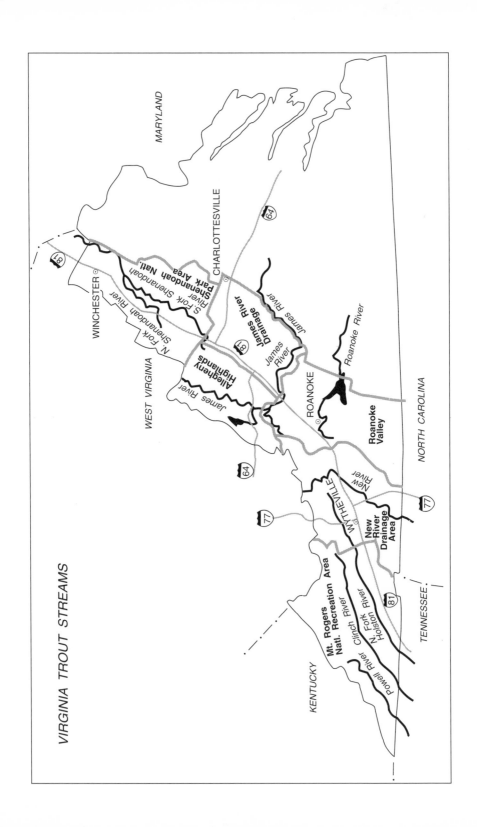

VIRGINIA TROUT STREAMS

Contents

ACKNOWLEDGMENTS

The author is happy to acknowledge six individuals who helped in the preparation of *Virginia Trout Streams:* Larry Mohn, Virginia fisheries biologist supervisor; Stephen Hiner, aquatic entomologist, Virginia Polytechnic Institute; Lew Thurman, skillful maker and user of split-bamboo fly rods; Beaver Shriver, trout guide; Ken Norton, photographer of Shenandoah National Park streams; and Mike Peters, tireless fishing partner.

H. S.

The author fishing a plunge pool in the Allegheny Highlands.

1

Introduction to Virginia Trout Streams

There are various estimates of the amount of trout water in Virginia, perhaps the most realistic being that published by the state's Department of Game and Inland Fisheries. They conservatively list 2,700 miles of trout water, 500 of it stocked plus 2,200 miles of wild trout streams. The brilliantly colored little native brook trout is one of Virginia's most precious resources, and as such is carefully nurtured in places like the Shenandoah National Park and on U.S. Forest Service land. That 2,200 miles of wild trout streams is one of the features which makes Virginia trout fishing unusual. Follow just about any stocked stream above the litter line, onto mountainsides steep enough to wrench thigh muscles, and eventually you will come upon near-virgin brook trout fishing.

For those accustomed to the classic streams of Pennsylvania, New England, or Montana, the climate of Virginia often comes as a surprise. Like many things in the South, trout fishing in the southern Appalachians sometimes has a touch of the surreal. You may find yourself fishing in mid-November in short sleeves, with a heavy swarm of Olive Quills rising from the stream.

Shirtsleeve fishing in November is a delight seldom experienced by northern anglers. Many Virginia stream-lashers prefer the solitude of fall fishing, when they own the stream except for a few bowhunters. There are cold days in autumn, of course, but even then fish become active at midday as the sun's warming effect takes over.

Virginia's low-altitude coastal plain to the east, plus the generally balmy climate, limit trout to the Allegheny and Blue Ridge mountains in the western part of the state. It is mainly on their high slopes that the water remains cold enough to maintain a year-round trout population. But between these two ranges is the unique limestone belt harboring the spring creeks so productive of healthy browns and rainbows. Both the Blue Ridge and Allegheny ranges are included in the catchall label, "Appalachian," which covers a whole netful of elevations in the eastern United States.

The primary objective of this book is to give careful directions for reaching some of Virginia's classic trout streams, including those that lie down unmarked "two-track" dirt roads. Secondly, the book gives a brief overview of what to expect when you get there. Third, it reflects a glimpse of the intense joy one may derive, not only from the angling, but also from just experiencing the Blue Ridge solitude one finds in Virginia's western mountains.

MANAGEMENT

The hardworking cadre of trout biologists employed by the state work closely with other state agencies and the federal government. They are a dedicated and sensitive group of people, spending increasingly more of their working hours protecting Virginia's fertile aquatic ecosystem against those whose actions would destroy some part of it. Some encroachment upon trout waters is inevitable, however, as Virginia's increasing population puts more pressure upon our water resources.

To the credit of the Department of Game and Inland Fisheries, and their helpers in Trout Unlimited, progress is being made. Virginians are waking up to the hard economic fact that trout fishing is an essential part of the state's tourism industry. If the trout environment suffers, the state's economy also suffers. Education of the public is an essential part of the state's program, in addition to following the basics of good trout management.

The three trout-management programs employed in Virginia are put-and-take stocking, protecting wild trout, and put-and-grow stocking. By far the most popular is put-and-take, since newly stocked trout are so easily caught, even by youngsters just beginning the sport. Unfortunately, tradition calls for a dialogue between adult put-'n'-takers that goes something like "Howdja do?" "Got m' limit," spoken with a knowing tilt of the head. That piece of dialogue has killed more good Virginia trout than disease, high water temperatures, acid rain, and poaching combined. On a stocking day, steely-eyed anglers with chain stringers dragging from their belts patrol the streams wielding spinning rods tipped with steel propellor-driven lures or bait, determined to get their limits. Within a short time the stream is virtually stripped clean of trout. Virginia fly-fishermen avoid these scenes as they would a hog-slaughtering.

Unannounced stocking was recently introduced on the Virginia trout scene. Without a doubt it has helped reduce the crowd waiting on the banks for trout to be dumped from the stocking truck. But there is still the underground network of ol' boys living near the hatchery who get on the phone to fishing buddies posthaste when they see a hatchery truck pulling out.

A second part of the state's trout-management program is the wild trout project. This encourages the reproducing populations of not only brook, but also rainbow and brown trout. Habitats are improved, and regulations protecting developing fish populations are enforced.

These wild trout demand cold, oxygenated water with a clean bottom and good fish cover. The most critical losses of trout in Virginia are caused by raised water temperatures resulting from the naturally warm climate and from drops in water level during the summer. Warming is not so much a problem in the high, shaded mountain streams, which remain below 70 degrees during hot spells. But removing the vegetation along even a short stretch of stream, through logging, farming, or development, can have disastrous results. Temperatures above the low 70s kill trout and encourage rough fish populations against which trout cannot compete.

Natural siltation, plus more unnatural changes, such as channelization, have cost Virginia many miles of trout streams. Silt cuts down on aquatic-insect populations, an important part of the trout's diet, and also makes reproduction difficult. Trout lay their eggs on gravel bottoms, after which the movement of cold, clean water over the eggs is a necessity. Even a quarter of an inch of silt covering newly hatched eggs can cause 100-percent mortality.

In Virginia today, the deterioration of trout habitat has been reversed, and a steady improvement in water quality is apparent. Another encouraging note: 80 percent of all Virginia wild trout are brook trout, the state's only true native trout. The growth rate of these brookies is phenomenal, eight to ten inches by the third year. This fast growth may be due to the longer growing season in Virginia as contrasted to the northern states. In fact, it's safe to say that the Old Dominion offers the best native brook fishing south of New England.

Unfortunately, there has been a tendency toward overfishing of popular wild trout streams. It is critical that wild fish spawn at least once before being creeled, and a seven-inch minimum size limit has helped the wild trout to reach spawning age in such streams. Trout, unlike warm-water fish such as perch and bass, have a very low ability to reproduce.

Perhaps the best solution to sustaining trout populations is encouraging the sportsman's willingness to catch and release. Although this philosophy has caught on in Pennsylvania and the New England states, very few Virginia anglers return their trout to freedom. When asked about this, a knowledgeable member of the Virginia Tech faculty replied, "I don't believe it's because Virginians are any less enlightened. It's just that no one has told them that catch-and-release is really the ethical way to go." It is interesting to note that Virginia bass fishermen have grasped the advantages of catch-and-release and are beginning to practice it. So there is hope that in the near future, instead of "Caught m' limit," Virginia trout anglers will be proud to say, "Caught and released *twice* my limit."

AUTHOR'S NOTE: I once heard an octogenarian in Highland County talk about his experience with trout as a child on the farm. In the evening, after chores were finished, his family would go to the bank of the river, light a fire, and bait up hickory poles. They would then pull in as many brook trout as possible, cleaning them and throwing them into a washtub to be used as a food staple. There may yet be some sentimental holdover of that agrarian attitude, even though there is no longer a rationale for it. Trout farms are now flourishing in western Virginia, producing a high quality of food fish under somewhat more ideal breeding conditions than the fragile ecosystem of the wild.

Fishing in Highland County, which has more than its share of outstanding trout streams.

On a more upbeat note, Virginia's 2,200 miles of wild trout water are today becoming free of the put-'n'-take mentality. Even some of the deepest backwoods anglers have begun adopting as part of their code the releasing of all the colorful little natives they hook. Hatchery trout are another matter.

One of the pure delights of Virginia fly-fishing is to follow a trail down some hickory ridge and hear the trickle of mountain water in the distance. Approaching closer, you can see the flash of sunlight on falling water. Parting the mountain laurel, you spot the dark shapes of brook trout hovering in some freestone basin, ready to dart away at the slightest movement. Prepare then to spend a day of Appalachian wild trout angling at its finest.

In addition to put-and-take and wild trout projects, there is a third primary management program known as "put-and-grow." This relatively small project involves the stocking of undersized trout which can be fished at a designated time under regulated conditions. Because of the high quality of trout fishing it provides, this program is growing in popularity and scope.

Two somewhat unusual management projects are found at Clinch Mountain and Crooked Creek. These are fee-fishing areas which provide put-and-take fishing with the added advantage that the streams are stocked several times weekly throughout the season. To fish these areas a daily permit is required, in addition to a valid state fishing license. Because of the encouragement they provide for young anglers and older beginners, these streams are included in this book. As usual in Virginia, you can trek upstream from the fee-fishers toward the sources and find wild trout fishing on these streams.

LICENSE REQUIREMENTS

All residents sixteen years of age and older are required to possess a state fishing license to fish for trout in Virginia. Persons who fish in designated waters stocked with catchable trout must have a separate trout license. A National Forest stamp, available wherever licenses are sold, is required for fishing in most waters within the George Washington and Thomas Jefferson National Forests. Refer to your fishing regulations pamphlet for exemptions.

When fishing in nondesignated trout waters, such as wild trout streams or special-regulation areas, you need only a state fishing license. Many of these special-regulation areas, however, require a signed permit card, obtained from Department of Inland Fisheries offices or from streamside landowners.

Out-of-state anglers fishing stocked waters need to purchase both the nonresident fishing license and the nonresident trout license. The nonresident fishing for wild trout or in special-regulation areas needs only a nonresident fishing license and the appropriate National Forest stamps plus special-regulation permits. A money-saver (depending on where you plan to fish) is the five-day license, which substitutes for the year-long nonresident license for five consecutive days. It's good only in unstocked trout waters.

The three fee-fishing (pay-as-you-go) areas described require only a state fishing license or a nonresident five-day license and a daily fishing permit which may be obtained on-site.

SPECIAL REGULATIONS

Distinct from the established trout-management waters are the special-regulation areas, which give hope for the future of fly-fishing in this state. Currently there are thirteen of these, all covered in this book, three of which are purely catch-and-release: North Fork Moorman's River, Stewart's Creek, and the Rapidan River. On the first two streams only single-hook artificial lures are permitted. On the Rapidan, only barbless single-hook artificial lures are permitted. In all three areas any fish caught must be released.

On the following ten streams, legal-sized fish may be kept, but the single-hook artificial-lure regulation applies, and all trout less than nine inches long must be returned to the water unharmed:

Conway River/Devil's Ditch (Greene County)
Smith Creek (Rockingham County)
Little Stony Creek (Giles County)
St. Mary's River (Augusta County)
Little Stony Creek (Shenandoah County)
Back Creek (Bath County)
North Creek (Botetourt County)
Whitetop Laurel/Green Cove Creek (Washington County)
Buffalo River (Amherst County)
Ramsey's Draft (Augusta County)

Another category of managed stream is trophy trout water, a concept new to Virginia. Here again only single-hook artificial lures may be used, but the difference is a creel restricted to no more than two fish per day, each over sixteen inches long. So far there are only three trophy streams: Smith Creek (Rockingham County), Mossy Creek (Augusta County), and Smith River (Henry County).

The Shenandoah National Park offers a wealth of special-regulation trout streams, within the park boundaries from Waynesboro to Front Royal. Generally, the regulations here call for single-hook artificial

Steve Hiner, entomologist at Virginia Polytechnic Institute, releasing a native brookie caught on a December morning.

lures only, a daily creel limit of five fish, and a minimum size of eight inches. The season opens the third Saturday in March and closes October 15. Variations to these rules will be posted at streamside. Six representative Shenandoah Park streams are described later in this book.

The regular trout season in Virginia runs from the third Saturday in March through February 1. The best fishing, theoretically, is from April 1 through mid-June, after which lowland streams have a lower and warmer flow. The resourceful angler can discover excellent fishing at any time of the year, however, by carefully picking his high-country streams and keeping a careful eye on the weather, whether in mid-August or mid-December.

Revenue from licenses provides around 800,000 stocked catchable trout per year, in addition to the fingerlings used in put-and-grow. Some idea of the program's scope is indicated by the thousands upon thousands of double-arrow signs marking stocked stretches. The signs denote waters open to public fishing according to an agreement between landowners and the Department of Game and Inland Fisheries. There are frequently stretches of stream so marked that are interrupted by posted stretches. Very rarely is any good Virginia trout water totally unsigned, and even then it's a good idea to check with the owner before fishing.

When special permits are needed for a particular stream, they may be obtained by sending your request with a self-addressed envelope to:

Virginia Department of Game and Inland Fisheries
4010 Broad Street
P.O. Box 11104
Richmond, Virginia 23230-1104

Or you may obtain permits from the local area office of The Department of Game and Inland Fisheries.

STREAM ACIDITY

In 1987 the Virginia Council of Trout Unlimited rounded up 200 volunteers from a cross section of environmental groups within the state. Their mission was to collect water samples from 349 streams during a scrambling two-week period. The samples were turned over to the University of Virginia for evaluation of chemical changes in these streams.

The results were not encouraging. Ninety-three percent of the 349 sampled trout streams were sensitive to acidification, while 10 percent were already acidic. Add to that the fact that rain in Virginia has reached a harmful level of acidity, with pH of 4.27, ten times more acid than normal. In fact, Virginia's Blue Ridge and Western Highlands receive more sulfate pollution than all of the northeastern United States.

Of all national parks in the country, the Shenandoah National Park receives the highest rate of sulfate deposition. The Great Smoky Mountains National Park comes in second. If this pollution level continues, the sensitive wild trout populations will decrease dramatically. Rainbows are the most sensitive species. The ability of the

Shenandoah Park streams to buffer acid has already been strained, and once this buffering capacity is gone, so will go Virginia's trout streams. The answer? It has been obvious for some time: reduce the levels of nitrogen oxide and sulfur dioxide being released into the atmosphere by fossil fuel burning, on both a local and national level. We can agree that further studies of acid rain are needed, but in the meantime, inertia is killing off one of Virginia's most valuable and colorful forms of wildlife.

HATCHES

The term "hatch" normally refers to *duns* or immature adults of aquatic insects reaching the surface. The four species of flies most noteworthy to Virginia anglers are mayflies, stoneflies, caddis flies, and the amorphous group called "midges." Significant hatches may be observed along the Blue Ridge seven or eight months out of the year, whenever the water temperature is above 50 degrees. A groggy Olive Quill has even been observed during Christmas week, looking as though it regretted the decision to emerge.

Nymphs are present beneath the surface virtually every day of the year, and thus a skillful wet-fly fisherman will naturally outperform the dry-fly angler, when their successes are averaged over a season. But when an active hatch is on the water, the dry fly is king. It's hard to beat the surface pop-and-splash drama of a day when spinners are swarming above the water, a spinner being a mating adult male, distinguished by its glassy clear wings. The so-called "spinner fall" refers mainly to the adult females falling exhausted with outstretched wings onto the surface to deposit their eggs. One Virginia veteran observer of spinner falls remarked, "If a trout won't take my dry fly, he's not worth catching anyhow." The prudent course may be to take along a mix of common wet and dry patterns, predominantly mayflies, to avoid being skunked on a given day.

The mayfly table below does not include every species found in Virginia. Rather, these are the species capably observed by Stephen W. Hiner, a member of the entomology department at Virginia Tech and an avid stream-lasher. He describes his listing as the mayfly "biggies" for fly-fishers matching the hatches in Virginia's trout streams:

MAYFLIES *(Ephemeroptera)*

Scientific Name	Common Name	Emergence	Location
Epeorus pleuralis	Quill Gordon	April	HF, MF
Paraleptophlebia spp.	Blue Quill	April	HF, MF
Epeorus vitreus	Gray Winged Yellow Quill	May	HF, MF
Stenonema vicarium	March Brown	May	HF, MF
Ephemerella dorothea	Pale Evening Dun (Sulfur)	May	All
Ephemerella berneri	Smith River Hendrickson	May	Smith River
Ephemera guttulata	Green Drake	May	All
Ephemerella rotunda	Light Hendrickson	May–June	L, T
Stenacron spp.	Light Cahill	June	HF, MF
Isonychia spp.	Mahogany Dun	June–Sept.	MF, LF
Trichorythodes spp.	Trico	Aug–Sept.	L
Baetis complex	Olive Quill	anytime	All
Drunella spp.	Blue Winged Olive	uncertain	T
Callibaetis spp.	Speckled Quill	summer–fall	Ponds

HF   = headwater freestone streams
MF   = midreach freestone streams
T   = tailwaters
L   = alkaline, limestone waters
spp. = reference is to various species within the genus named

The Pale Evening or Sulfur Dun is one of the more significant Virginia mayflies. It is found on all stream types and plays a key role in the Shenandoah National Park stream ecosystem. It is a generally exciting and dependable hatch in the Appalachians.

The Green Drake, prolific in more northern latitudes, isn't a big hatch in Virginia, though some anglers consider it essential on the Whitetop Laurel.

Mahogany Duns are probably more important in the nymph than the dun stage. The nymphs crawl out of the water onto stones and bridge supports, making the dun less available to fish. The Lead-Winged Coachman best approximates it.

The Speckled Quill occurs in every "trout pond" in Virginia, sometimes in great numbers. It's usually most active in late summer and fall.

Below the Gathright Dam on the Jackson River, at least two species of Blue Winged Olives occur in staggering numbers. They are probably one reason this stretch of water is becoming one the state's most successful stock-and-grow projects.

Much of the mayfly activity in Virginia is still under active study, and more will be known as fly-fishing gains in popularity here. There will probably never be the great volume of insect lore recorded in states such as Pennsylvania, though. There is no counterpart here to Charlie Meck's sharp-eyed cadre of Pennsylvania bugwatchers armed with notebook and pencil. There are, however, some highly authoritative academic entomologists who have added to the literature and corrected some taxonomic errors in the mayfly arena, in particular Reese Voshell, professor of entomology and aquatic insect study at Virginia Tech, and Boris Kondratieff, who is now at Colorado State. Kondratieff was one of Voshell's first graduate students at Tech during the early eighties, when they worked together on an extensive study of aquatic insects along the Blue Ridge watersheds.

STONEFLIES *(Plecoptera)*

There have been 149 species of stoneflies reported in Virginia, the highest number from any state. By contrast 77 species have been reported in Kentucky, 130 in North Carolina, and 106 in West Virginia. The wealth of stoneflies in Virginia is due to the variety of topography found here—including five major types, ranging from the Coastal Plain to Piedmont Plateau through Blue Ridge, Ridge and Valley, and most importantly, Appalachian Plateau.

Add to that eight major river basins, including the New River, second oldest river on earth next to the Nile. These watersheds drain from a height of 5,720 feet atop Mount Rogers, down to the Coastal Plain's sea level. There are eighty species of stoneflies in the central Appalachians and Piedmont Plateau foothills alone. It's no wonder biologists rank this area one of the richest in North America in terms of different plant and animal species.

Virginia native trout have been the partakers in a stonefly feast since many millennia before the arrival of Sir Walter Raleigh. Despite this bonanza of stonefly species, however, there are really only four basic stonefly patterns Virginia fly-fishers need to concentrate upon:

—*Winter and spring stoneflies*, which continue to emerge through December. Just before Christmas holidays, Smith River browns have been observed feeding on the adults.

—*Giant stoneflies* are found in most headwater streams. During its nymph stage it is best imitated with the black stone nymph, a real gulp for brookies.

—*Common stoneflies* live up to their name in both small and medium-sized Virginia freestone streams. They are the most colorful of the stoneflies, occurring in mottled patterns of black, brown, and yellow. Many of the more popular realistic patterns are tied to imitate common stoneflies.

—*The little yellow stonefly*, which is a branch of the *Perlodidae* family, becomes most significant as an adult in freestone headwater streams during May through July.

CADDIS FLIES *(Trichoptera)*

The two streams in Virginia with best caddis fly potential are the Smith and Jackson, the former having the most prolific hatches, and the Jackson providing the greater variety.

The net-spinner caddis flies include the Spotted Sedge and Little Sister Sedge. These occur in most waters, and emerge from April through July. Among the tube case makers, there are a couple of caddis fly genera worth mentioning. One is the Autumn Mottled Sedge. It emerges around September and October. The Plain Brown Sedge and American Grannom are a couple of other spring-emerging caddis flies of localized importance in certain freestone streams.

MIDGES

Although the label "midge" is commonly applied to the small slappable insects frequenting streams and the anatomies of trout anglers, there is only one true midge family, the *Chironomidae*. Blackflies and crane flies are often mistakenly called midges, along with some of the tinier species of mayflies, and there are many midges which defy any systematic labeling.

These gnatty species are common to Virginia streams and add much to the pleasure of all Virginia anglers—including that peculiar breed who crunches through fringes of January ice. Midges are all quite small and require a special kind of fishing tactic which Stephen Hiner labels "insane behavior," referring to the reduction of everything to its smallest common denominator: light line, 6X tippet, Number 20 or Number 22 flies. Even if you have excellent vision, you'll find some craziness involved in midge fishing, because getting close enough to see such a mini-fly means standing very close indeed to the fish.

TERRESTRIALS

During certain times of the year every Virginia trout stream is dependent upon terrestrials—either partially or completely—for fish forage. Certain streams on certain late summer days must be fished exclusively with terrestrials. Mossy Creek during hopper time is an outstanding example.

One unique feeding pattern observed involves trout under dense overhangs taking only specific terrestrials, such as beetles or ants, while their brethren in midstream are feeding on aquatic insects. Several, not all, of the key Virginia terrestrials are: hoppers, crickets, leafhoppers, beetles, moths, inchworms, and ants.

Suppose none of the above insect patterns seems to be moving on a stream? One good way to test trout activity is with an Adams Number 18, fished as an attractor. If the feeding action on a particular day is wet all the way, a Muddler Minnow 16 or 18 worked with a vibration from the wrist is sometimes an accurate test of the day's angling potential.

SAFETY

COLD WEATHER HAZARDS

Slipping and taking a dunking in electrifyingly cold trout water is one of the minor discomforts of summertime angling. On an October day when the temperature is around 45 degrees, it becomes a matter of somewhat more than discomfort. Many anglers do not realize that hypothermia can result from air temperatures in the 40s. After thrashing out of an icy plunge pool in autumn or winter, you can have more than just chattering teeth. After the onset of severe shivering, a dunking victim may have difficulty walking and speaking. Next comes drowsiness and progressive confusion, sometimes even leading to hallucination. In severe cases there may be cardiac arrest.

For a mild hypothermia, with a body temperature down in the 90–95 degree range, the condition may not seem serious. The victim is conscious, fairly alert, and shivering. A little exercise, walking briskly and flailing the arms, should help start the blood flowing. But even a mild drop in temperature can lead to some disorientation. That increasing feeling of confusion makes finding your way out of some remote native trout stream with little or no trail a more serious matter. With a breeze blowing and a drop in temperature as shadows lengthen, soaking wet clothing becomes a critical health problem.

Prevention is always best, and wearing felt soles on your waders can often prevent a bone-jarring wet back flip. In cool weather wear insulated waders or thermal underwear, or both. A wading staff does not have to be an elaborate and costly piece of hardware. A hickory stick with a hole drilled in the head to accommodate a loop of thong, plus a rubber cane tip, will work fine. Wading across the current in a spring freshet often requires that tripodal support from a good staff firmly placed downstream. With a thong sufficient to fit over the head, it can be slung out of the way until needed by even the most macho image-conscious stream-lasher.

Despite all precautions, you're going to fall in. There's never any doubt it will happen, usually when you have just placed your boot on what appears to be the most secure and dry stone in the stream.

Whoops! Now you're in up to your armpits, and it's Virginia Appalachian Spring cold. What now? After you've crawled out on the bank, it's time to take from your fishing vest that medicine vial of strike-anywhere matches dipped in paraffin. It helps that the vial top was also sealed with melted paraffin. Or you may prefer a small butane lighter, sealed in a Ziploc bag with some bottle-cap candles.

Whatever the method, start a fire, fast, with the usual precautions of a stone ring surrounded by bare ground. Putting modesty aside, wring out at least some of the wet clothing and hang it by the fire. When your teeth have stopped playing *Night on Bald Mountain,* and your clothes are damp but warm enough to put back on, head back to your vehicle. There you will find that complete change of dry clothing you always carry, even in July. You do, don't you? Anyone who's really needed a dry set of clothing, including underdrawers, is never again without them. Alcoholic beverages are out following a soaking, as they lower body temperature. On the other hand, a thermos of hot coffee on the tailgate will help with both morale and physical discomfort.

Most household fever thermometers don't register below 94 degrees and may hide a case of even mild hypothermia. When hypothermia progresses without treatment, confusion gives way to unconsciousness accompanied by shock. It's then a life-or-death situation. If you encounter someone suffering from obviously prolonged exposure, he or she should be immediately transported to the nearest medical facility with as little jostling as possible. Severe hypothermia is a tricky matter, and the difficult treatment should be attempted by a lay person only if no medical help is available. It involves warmth, in any form, including blankets, car heater, sleeping bag, and even body-to-body transfer of heat.

In Virginia's western mountains, you may be well over an hour's walk from your vehicle, whether in a federal park preserve or a national forest primitive area. In fact, that's where you'll find the best native brook trout fishing. Before leaving the pavement, always notify someone where you will be and when. Shenandoah National Park rangers urge you to inform them before hiking in to one of their streams alone—and it makes good sense. Crawling four miles with hypothermia or a fractured leg is much less desirable than just waiting for help to come when you don't show up back at your vehicle.

POISONOUS SNAKES

The southern Appalachians are home to only two species of poisonous snakes, the timber rattler and the copperhead. Although it is not as irritable or venomous as its western diamondback cousin, the timber rattler's bite is much more serious than that of the copperhead. There is no recent history of anyone's dying from the bite of a copperhead in Virginia. Rattlers are much less commonly encountered than copperheads, though state Inland Fisheries field workers don't agree that holds true in trout stream terrain. Both of these venomous species are slow-moving and anxious to get out of your way.

Check with local landowners or park personnel to see if there has been a problem with venomous snakes on the stream you're planning to fish. If so, either change your plans or be extra cautious where you step. In snake country, the wading staff doubles as a probe for poking vigorously into high grass or rock piles before taking a blind step. A good staff will also serve as a warning when rapped smartly on the stones or thrashed against the weeds. Most of the time snakes will depart when given such a warning. An exception is a snake caught out of its den by a cool snap, when it will be sluggish and less likely to move away. That may be a good time to stay in midstream.

There are thirty species of snakes in Virginia, many of which are often mistaken for copperheads. One of the startling copperhead lookalikes on trout streams are northern water snakes, which proliferate there. These are nonvenomous, but highly destructive to trout particularly at low water. If the water snakes are actively feeding, you may as well leave the stream.

There's so much medical controversy surrounding the use of tourniquets, cut-and-suck snakebite kits, ice packs, and other treatment methods that it's hard to distinguish which, if any, is the preferred treatment. Few physicians disagree, however, with immobilizing the bite victim and carrying him or her to a medical facility equipped with antivenin as rapidly as possible.

TICKS

As if Rocky Mountain spotted fever weren't enough, a new tick hazard has invaded the woods, Lyme disease. Both ailments may be contracted in Virginia's forests, although an official at the state's Department of Health states, "There is a very small risk of contracting the disease [Lyme] here." In 1989 the department recorded only fifty-four cases. The majority of these were on the Eastern Shore's coastal area and the Piedmont flatlands, rather than the mountains. Not to minimize the seriousness of Lyme's, but with all the overblown publicity, there is need for a realistic perspective.

Luckily, scientists have accumulated a great deal of knowledge about this disease since it was first discovered in Lyme, Connecticut, in 1976. Caused by a tick-borne spirochete bacteria, *Borrelia burgdorferi,* like any bacterial disease it can be cured by antibiotics, preferably high doses in the early stages. The two ticks most likely to carry Lyme's in Virginia are the *Ixodes dammini,* and the more prevalent *Ixodes scapulari,* both tiny enough to be comfortable on the head of a pin.

Because the carriers are smaller than any ticks we are accustomed to, it is best to wear light-colored clothing on which they may be spotted more easily. Wear long-sleeved shirts, preferably tight around the wrists. Insect repellent works on these small blood-suckers, especially DEET in concentrations of 30 percent or more.

Most active in Virginia in May through October, ticks may also be found here up through late fall because of the warm winters. It's a good idea for you and your fishing partner to check one another's clothes frequently. When you get home strip down and put your clothes into the washer as soon as possible. Check yourself over for tiny crawlers, and then scrub down thoroughly in the shower.

If in spite of these precautions you find a tick biting you, gently remove it by pulling upward with tweezers or facial tissue. Take care not to break it off, and don't bother with matches, Vaseline, or some of the other jackleg methods formerly recommended. Save the tick in a jar of alcohol in case you begin showing any of the Lyme disease symptoms.

During the first stage of the illness there is the classic rash which expands slowly and fades in the center, giving it a bull's-eye appearance. You may also get flulike first-stage symptoms: slight fever, stiff muscles, fatigue, headaches, and swollen lymph nodes. It may take several days to weeks for these to appear, and then take care. The symptoms vanish, lulling you into thinking there's no problem. Treatment is much more effective during this first stage, so don't ignore the symptoms. Second-stage symptoms appear weeks or even months later. Now you may have headaches, stiff neck, sleeplessness, and lack of coordination. Watch for dizziness, weakness, and irregular heartbeat, all and any of which may disappear and reappear without warning. The third stage appears as chronic arthritis, especially of the knees, shoulders, and wrists. There may be serious neurological problems as well. The invasion of Lyme disease into internal organs such as the brain or heart may be fatal unless treated with massive doses of intravenous penicillin. Even when confined to the joints, the bacteria may cause an immune response resulting in permanent crippling polyarthritis.

More prevalent than Lyme disease, but less talked about, is Rocky Mountain spotted fever, carried by the larger wood tick. Symptoms are fever, rash, generalized aches and pains, and headache. See a physician if any of these occurs after a tick bite.

Be aware of Lyme's and Rocky Mountain spotted fever, but don't listen to the hysteria that surrounds them, and know enough about the diseases to take precautions against catching them. Then go out and enjoy the hopper season along Virginia's trout streams, including the ones with brushy banks.

EQUIPMENT

Fly-fishing in Virginia is not an elitist sport requiring an array of expensive gear. If you have inherited a fine old split bamboo rod, or even a thirty-year-old Shakespeare Wonderod, be grateful and be careful, but experience the joy of using it. In shopping for a new rod, the choice should be dictated by the type of water on which it will be used. In the western Appalachians, we are concerned mainly with small streams, often having a series of rapids, falls, and plunge pools. Paradoxically, a longer rod, 7 or 7½ feet, works best on these

There are some good trout holes beneath this waterfall in the Allegheny Highlands.

mountain waters. A shorter rod requires approaching closer, losing the advantage of stealth. With a 7-footer carrying a lively, but not too soft tip, your fly can be eased through a hole in the overhanging laurel or rhododendron and dropped upstream of a feeding brookie.

The choice of a rod, or any other fly-fishing equipment, is highly personal. Some skilled anglers favor a featherweight little bamboo wand less than six feet long, with which they have learned to place a fly accurately at enough distance to avoid alarming the fish. If you are just beginning, try a number of combinations—long and short—to see which fits your style best. Most tackle shops will loan equipment, or better yet, furnish professional trout guides with an assortment of rods and lines.

Perhaps the most confusing choice for the fly-fisher is line. From a dazzling array of weights, colors, tapers, and synthetic materials, you are expected to choose just the right one. As a rule of thumb, the rod, plus the size of flies you favor, will narrow down the choice. Be prepared to down-size to Number 20 flies on days when the fish spurn your larger offerings. Fly lines run from Number 1 to 14, with the smaller numbers denoting lighter and finer lines. Size 4 or less line will drop even a tiny Number 20 Adams on the water in a gentle and lifelike manner. Size 6 line has enough heft to carry larger streamers and hoppers on big brown trout waters and will also get by handling smaller flies adequately when necessary.

The choice of floating or sinking line may be dictated by where the trout are feeding on a particular day. Because it feels slightly heavier on the rod than the floating variety, a sinking line may be a few grains lighter than the corresponding number of floating line. One answer to the float-*vs.*-sink choice is to load two reels, one with each type, and switch reels on the stream as dictated by where the trout are feeding that day.

Line taper is another consideration. Some beginners start with an untapered, or level line, which will work fine. Later, when they have more feeling for the finer points, a double taper is a good choice, that is, a line tapered at both ends. It's the most economical because when one end starts to wear, you can just swap to the other end, doubling the life of your line. The belly, or middle section, seldom shows any appreciable wear.

What about color? You have a choice of lines ranging from mahogany through blue, green, yellow, orange, and white. You also have your choice of many highly vocal opinions on line color. Some anglers swear by floating green, claiming it blends in with the overhead vegetation. Others claim that white will scare fish away. Maybe so, but a white line is always visible to you, and adding on the length of the leader, you can calculate just where even the tiniest fly is located on the water if you can see your line. A compromise here is an off-white or light tan line, which still offers visibility without calling attention to itself. These lighter colors are used by some experienced trout guides in Virginia, with consistent success.

Some lightweight line users favor the weight-forward over the double-tapered line, claiming it gives them a longer cast faster, and works well into the wind. For the small Virginia streams, however, a double-taper works fine, with the small difference in weight forward not really mattering on a Number 4 through 6 line. And in some cases the line debate becomes academic, since short casting room requires a dependence upon the eight or ten feet of monofilament leader.

On a given day, the length and weight of your leader may have the greatest influence upon success and failure. For small dry flies, a knotted taper starting from a .02-inch butt and going down to at least 5X is best. For some of the more fickle feeders, a 6X is favored by some anglers, even with the frail tippet's tendency to curl. When you are fishing a sinking line, attaching a fluorescent marker to your leader will improve chances of detecting a subtle underwater tug.

Fly reels are sometimes taken for granted, looked upon as spools for storing line. With reels as elsewhere, however, there are always better and worse. Some cheaper models allow the line to jam up between the spool and sides. If you've just hooked that citation brown who's eluded you all season, and he's headed for underwater brush, a jammed reel means goodbye. Also take a look at the starting drag, since that same big brown will break the leader without a light starting drag.

Hip boots are adequate for wading on most Virginia mountain streams, and there may be August days when it's a relief to step out into midstream shod only in shorts and felt-soled wading shoes. On some of the larger streams, such as the Jackson and the Smith, chest waders are necessary. On a frosty day, chest waders can be a boon if you slip and fall into even a small stream. Yes, Virginia, there is some of the world's slipperiest algae on your rocks, even during cold weather. A dry backside sometimes makes carrying the extra weight of insulated chest waders worthwhile. Speaking of which, felt soles are well worth whatever they may cost, in terms of fewer bruises or broken bones.

One very essential piece of gear is a set of surgical forceps, dangling from your fishing vest. For removing a hook quickly without harming the trout, these are indispensable. Many expert anglers nowadays use their forceps so deftly that they never have to touch the fish, and have given up landing nets in favor of an accurate grab of the hook by their forceps while the trout is still waterborne.

Fishing vests, front or rear-loaded fly carriers, and fishing hats are a matter of personal choice, with unlimited variety. It may be wise to remember, however, that Virginia landowners are mostly mountain-grown farmers. To approach them asking permission to fish, while wearing a getup worth of Stewart Granger, the Great White Angler, may not be the wisest way to go.

In choosing fly-fishing equipment, one rule to keep in mind is that there are few rules. The cookbook approach is simply not appropriate, and it's best to experiment with rods, lines, leaders, and all the other paraphernalia of trout angling until you're comfortable with what you have.

MAPS AND HIGHWAY DIRECTIONS

This book contains maps of each of the six regions covered, plus individual maps of some of the most important stream. Often, however, you will find it useful to refer to more detailed topographic maps.

Traditionally the topographic maps published by the United States Geological Survey (USGS) have been the most useful sources of information for anglers. The USGS has published several series, but the commonest series today in Virginia is the 7½ minute series, with a scale of one inch per 2,000 feet. These maps can tell a great deal about a stream—whether it flows through open or forested terrain, how steeply it drops, where tributaries enter. They can also help you find the easiest access to streams by showing roads, trails, power line cuts, etc. USGS maps have their drawbacks as well, however, particularly the fact that they are sometimes out of date and do not show some current trails and landmarks. Nevertheless, they remain important tools for anglers, and the appropriate 7½ minute series USGS quadrangle is listed at the beginning of each stream description.

Individual USGS maps are available at some book and sporting goods stores and can also be ordered from:

Distribution Branch
United States Geological Survey
Box 25286
Federal Center
Denver, Colorado 80225
(303) 236-7477

This office will also provide, free of charge, an index and catalogue of USGS maps of Virginia.

The best and most convenient collection of topographic maps in one volume is the *Virginia Atlas and Gazetteer*. It is available in most sporting goods stores for $12.95 or may be ordered from:

The DeLorme Mapping Company
P.O. Box 298
Freeport, Maine 04032
(207) 865-4171

DeLorme map references are also given for each stream described.

Ordinary road maps, published by the state of Virginia, oil companies, or automobile clubs, can also help provide stream access information. The Virginia Department of Transportation, 1401 East Broad Street, Richmond, Virginia 23219, publishes inexpensive county road maps which can be quite useful to anglers.

Throughout the text, highways and roads are indicated by the following letter symbols:

I   = Interstate
US   = U.S. Highway
VA   = State highway
VA(s)   = Secondary State Highway
FR   = National Forest Road

2

Shenandoah National Park Area

The 200,000 acres of hardwood forest within the park boundaries includes one of the few sizable areas of wild trout habitat in the eastern U.S. Since it's located only a short distance from Washington, D.C., Baltimore, and other large metropolitan areas, the park and its environs play host to millions of visitors each year. In spite of this pressure, the native brook trout population is thriving, due to careful management and cooperation from the angling public. There are approximately thirty managed streams, with a total of over ninety streams within the total brook trout ecosystem. Several streams, such as the Rapidan, are designated catch-and-release, but the concept of carefully handling and releasing fish is fostered within the entire fishery.

These picturesque freestone mountain streams do not contain an abundance of food, particularly when compared to Virginia's rich limestone spring waters. The lack of natural foods keeps the trout in the Shenandoah Park constantly on the move in search of the best feeding station, with the largest fish occupying the most rewarding spots. This constant rotation of hungry fish makes for some exciting action and furnishes enough nourishment to keep the brookies thriving and growing.

For the most part these are hike-in fishing locations, requiring a little foresight in putting together equipment which is easily packed down

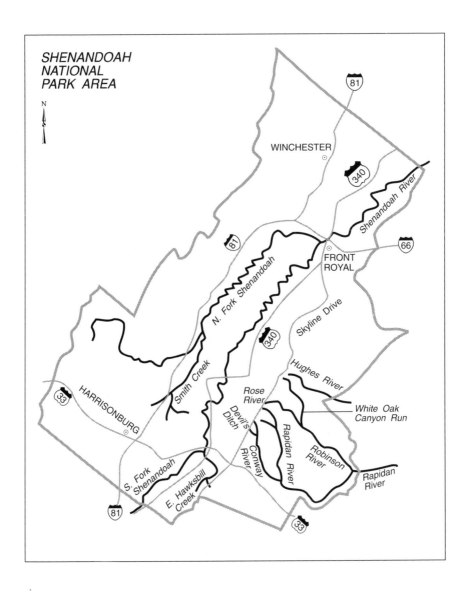

fairly steep trails—and what is even more important, back up again.

The two visitor information centers within the park offer maps and advice on current fishing conditions on specific streams. Since certain fisheries are closed during low water, it is always a good idea to check before hiking in. Another source of fishing data on the park is the book *Trout Fishing in the Shenandoah National Park,* by Harry Murray (Edinburg, Virginia: Shenandoah Publishing Company, 1989). This publication gives detailed directions on which trails to follow from the Skyline Drive down to twenty-eight streams and also on how to reach them from the lower park boundary. The following section covers six of the best Shenandoah Park waters, plus nearby Smith Creek, presenting a cross section of stream types from the robust White Oak Canyon Run to the reclusive East Hawksbill Creek. The southernmost portion of the park is within the James River Drainage, and two of the best streams in that area (Meadow Run and the North Fork of the Moorman's River) are described in Chapter 4.

CONWAY RIVER / DEVIL'S DITCH

Stream type: Freestone • USGS Fletcher • DeLorme 68

This stream's upper reaches flow through the Shenandoah National Park, and the regulations governing the park's wild brook trout population apply. Lower down, the Conway and its major tributary, Devil's Ditch, lie within the Rapidan Wildlife Management Area. Here special regulations are in effect, requiring single-hook artificial lures with a creel limit of six fish of nine inches or more. All fish less than nine inches must be returned unharmed.

The Conway River Road follows the stream for most of its length, providing easy access. A typical Shenandoah range fishery, it's an attractive stream, well worth a visit. It suffers during midsummer droughts, but can be fished productively during the spring and fall, sometimes even well into December. Be prepared for a full day of stream-lashing on the Conway with firm regrets when dusk deepens enough to make even a parachute fly invisible. The Light Cahill hatch in May calls for a matching Number 14 dry and nymph. The first major hatch here, as on most Shenandoah Park streams, is the Quill Gordon in March and April, calling for Number 14 or 12 dry or nymphs. When fly hatches die down in summer and fall, keep a sharp eye for terrestrial fill-ins: crickets, hoppers, beetles, and both black and red ants.

Adult brook trout in the upper reaches range from seven to eleven inches, on the average. There are healthy wild brown trout scattered through the lower reaches, with some occasional rod-benders exceeding twenty inches.

Directions: The primary access is VA(s) 667 through the town of Fletcher. Northbound from US 29, turn west onto US 33 to Stanardsville. There turn right onto VA(s) 230, for 3 miles, then left onto VA(s) 667 which parallels the Conway upstream into the Rapidan Wildlife Management Area, on past the intersection of Devil's Ditch.

EAST HAWKSBILL CREEK

STREAM TYPE: Freestone • USGS Big Meadows • DeLorme 74

For the mountain stream purist who wants absolute solitude along with his native trout fishing, the East Hawksbill has much to offer. Like most precious commodities, however, the rare solitude carries a high price. After descending the precipitous mountainside and fishing all day, you still have that teeth-clenching climb back to the top to be reckoned with. On the plus side, the stream is small enough to be fished without hip waders, so you don't need their added weight.

After navigating down the mountainside for around an hour, you hear the reassuring sound of falling water ahead, and through the trees you'll see the mini-waterfalls of the East Hawksbill. The stream's upper section offers few trout, so before assembling your fly rod it's a good idea to hike down to where the gradient is a little gentler. Here there are more waterfalls and rapids, but with deeper green granite bowls beneath them containing more frequent trout shapes.

The rapid water discourages aquatic insects to some degree, but even in late October a small, hardy colony of mayflies has been spotted, looking a little wobbly at the prospect of being born into Indian Summer. The usual terrestrials, Number 16 red and black ants plus small beetles and black gnats, also may stir up some action. It's one of those streams with overhanging limbs through which you find a space

Thanks to careful management, the freestone mountain streams in
Shenandoah National Park contain a thriving brook trout population.

to insert your rod, then dap the fly against a rock with a likely-looking dark shadow beneath it.

It is recommended that you time your fishing on the East Hawksbill to give you plenty of daylight for the trip back up the mountain. There's no public access at the lower end. It's also a good idea to have a companion with you, as much of the trail requires stepping from boulder to boulder, with the good possibility of a sprained ankle. Trekking to the East Hawksbill isn't easy by any standards, but then, you won't find any boot tracks or beverage cans along the stream. Even if you don't hook an abundance of trout, this may still become your most memorable fishing experience in the Shenandoah Park.

Directions: This stream is reached from the Hawksbill Gap parking area, between Skyline Drive milepost 45 and 46. The concrete marker at the trailhead indicates the lower Hawksbill Trail down the west side of the Shenandoah Range. Do not take this more heavily used footpath on the left. Go 20 feet to the right and follow that connector across the Appalachian Trail about 200 feet down. This connector trail then continues to a running water standpipe indicated as "Spring" on the marker. From there down to the stream a park ranger reported there is a wagon road. Good luck! The uppermost reaches of East Hawksbill, a spring branch, follows a mile-long rock slide at a 40-degree angle down, conjuring up the image of a potato wagon teetering over the brink and bouncing out of control three times to the bottom. There may be the trace of a wagon road several hundred yards to the right of the spring branch, but rainstorms and hurricanes have pretty well obliterated it. A safer bet is to follow the headwater down to the point at which the Hawksbill begins to look like a trout stream.

HUGHES RIVER

Stream type: Freestone • USGS Old Rag Mountain
DeLorme 74

Fishing the Hughes River on a good day can fulfill the greatest expectations of Shenandoah native trout fishing. These are not large brookies, but they are scrappy and so colorful they look like cylindrical autumn maple leaves lying on the bottom. To dismiss these fish as too minuscule to be worthy is like dismissing Sugar Ray Leonard as too small to be a fighter. And occasionally there is a wily native heavyweight with lip scars to prove how many seasons he has survived.

The Hughes is a deceptive stream, with long shallow pools which seem devoid of life. But a black-bodied Number 18 parachute fly dropped on these insignificant-looking flats can produce instant small explosions of red and gold. The farther downstream you fish, the bigger the water, with man-sized feeder streams along the way. Paradoxically, the larger fish, and more of them, seem to occur upstream all the way to the Corbin Cabin, a restored settler's home, identical to most Appalachian log originals still standing. This heavy upstream population may be due to less fishing pressure farther from the road. Since it's nearly two miles from the Skyline Drive, with a taxing uphill climb after fishing, the upper Hughes is not for everyone. Even those with a taste for solitary fishing should have had their annual physicals fairly recently. The Nicholson Hollow Trail is not a difficult walk, but it definitely is uphill all the way back, and steeply so at that.

A mile or so below the Corbin Cabin the gradient is steeper with fewer quiet pools, thus calling for slightly different tactics. A Number 16 black ant, cast (intentionally) onto the side of a boulder and then coaxed into the rapids, closely approximates one feeding pattern. When these fish are hungry, however, almost anything that touches the water from any angle is attacked instantly. In the spring with active hatches about, Light Cahill or Hendrickson Number 16s may attract more discriminating feeders.

Regardless of the season, as with any native stream, delicate changes may make the difference. As an example, casting with a 5X leader, a perfectly respectable practice, may produce zero strikes. But changing to a Number 5.5 or 6 leader on a given day may break the silence instantly. Believe it or not, switching from a black to a red ant fished dry can wake up dormant trout appetites. On these Shenandoah streams it is always a good idea to see what is flying or crawling, and to turn over an underwater stone or two for a nymph check.

Regardless of the entomological population, a Muddler Minnow may turn the trick. Fishing for native trout on the Hughes, or anywhere for that matter, is seldom a predictable science, despite what merchandisers of fly-fishing equipment would have us believe. The river may have unstoppable action, with small red-and-gold thunderbolts striking at every pool, while only a few miles away, on a similar stream such as the Rose River, there's no sign of trout.

Since the Shenandoah is strictly a no-hunting park, you will sometimes get the distinct feeling you're being watched on the Hughes. A look across the river may disclose a doe grazing on the opposite bank, with only an occasional diffident glance at the odd human waving his 7½-foot sapling at the water.

AUTHOR'S NOTE: On a summery October 4, I found myself on the Hughes River after an essentially fruitless morning on other streams in the Shenandoah Park. To my surprise, the colorful little Hughes River brookies smashed everything I offered them, wet or dry. I could do no wrong, and after releasing twenty autumnally crimson-and-gold brookies, I lost count. The farther upstream I moved, the more intense the action, which is often the case with these Shenandoah streams.

The Hughes River offers good native trout fishing almost any time, but it's a perfect stream for a warm late Autumn or Indian Summer day. It's not necessary to arrive early in the morning, and in fact at that time of the year midmorning may be the ideal condition, with the water warming up and even some hardy hatches appearing. The one problem is confusion created by multicolored leaves floating downstream, making your fly more difficult to single out. Switching to wets can sometimes clear up the confusion. And the walk back up the mountainside on a brisk autumn evening is much less demanding than during the sweaty season.

Directions: The best way to reach this stream is from above, between Skyline Drive mileposts 38 and 39. Park at the Stony Man Overlook and take the Nicholson Hollow Trail, which is 300 yards north of the parking area. This takes you 1.8 miles down the mountainside, over a feeder stream, and to the Hughes. Fishing is best at and below the Corbin Cabin.

Falls such as this one keep Shenandoah Park streams well oxygenated in the summer.

The Hughes River can also be reached from below, by taking VA(s) 600 through the town of Nethers past the Old Rag Mountain parking area. Around a mile farther is a small pull-off, and from there the Nicholson Hollow Trail follows the stream for the most part, straying away from the water occasionally. The upper stretch of this stream provides better action.

RAPIDAN RIVER

STREAM TYPE: Freestone • USGS Fletcher • DeLORME 68

Special restrictions on fishing (see below) have preserved a fair population of Rapidan brook trout, the smaller of which are easily seen. Larger fish are more wary and hook-wise, and the use of 6X leader is recommended, particularly at times of low water.

Hiking in to the Rapidan's headwaters at Camp Hoover from above takes around half an hour, most of it downhill. The perfectly preserved sixty-year-old camp buildings are reserved for use by members of Congress and their staffs, some of whom emulate President Herbert Hoover, who loved to get away from Washington and fish for brook trout in the Rapidan. The president was said to have a "quick wrist," certainly an asset, though not a necessity, on this stair-step boulder-and-pool section of the stream. As you look down the mountainside, the stream is hidden by the chunks of granite marking its passage for a steep quarter of a mile. The hike in and out is part of the experience of fishing this historic stream, and you're likely to startle deer from their fern beds or a family of wild turkeys crossing the trail.

For the pure fly-fishing experience, the lower and central portions downstream may be driven to. The ford connecting these two stretches is tricky, however, and a high-clearance four-wheel-drive vehicle may save you a midstream stranding miles from any phone. The catch-and-release regulations also apply to the central and lower Rapidan.

Number 16 black beetles and dry ants, red or black, are productive. There is also a rusty-colored fly called the Mr. Rapidan, tied locally in sizes 12 through 18, which is a warm-weather favorite. Hatches of reddish insects, dead ringers for the Mr. Rapidan, may occasionally be seen flitting on the surface. Depending on the time of year, nymphs, streamers, and hatch-matched dry flies are successful.

Special Regulations: Below the bridge at Camp Hoover, this is catch-and-release water: fishing restricted to artificial flies or lures with single, barbless hooks (note: below the Shenandoah National Park boundary, barbed hooks are permitted); all trout must be handled carefully and returned immediately to the water; possession of trout,

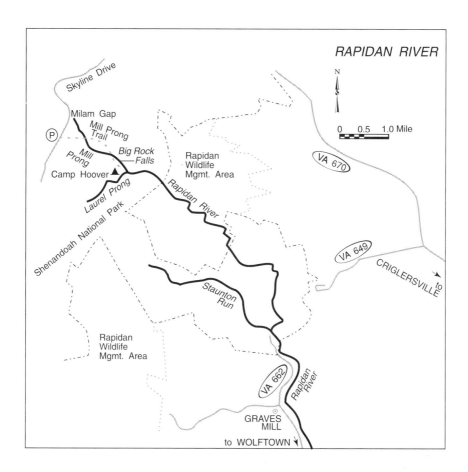

of any size, is illegal. Game fish of other species may be kept, subject to regulations applying to various species in Virginia waters generally.

Directions: To reach the Camp Hoover stream access from the Skyline Drive, it is necessary to hike approximately two miles on a moderately difficult trail. Park at the Milam Gap area, between mileposts 52 and 53 of the Skyline Drive. Cross the highway and take the Appalachian Trail, blazed with white, which immediately intersects with Mill Prong Trail, blazed with blue. Follow that to the horse trail, where the blazes become yellow, leading past Big Rock Falls to Camp Hoover. Just below the camp where Laurel and Mill Prongs join, regulated fishing on the Rapidan begins.

From below, access to the central portion of the Rapidan is via VA(s) 649/670 from Criglersville. The lower portion is reached by VA(s) 662 from Graves Mill. From the locked gate on the Rapidan Road to Camp Hoover is around a mile and a half.

ROSE RIVER

Stream type: Freestone • USGS Big Meadows • DeLorme 68, 74

More deserving of the surname River than most other similarly labeled Shenandoah Park streams, the Rose empties out of the park with a respectable volume of water. Driving up VA(s) 670, you see stocking signs along the way, with numerous spin fishermen taking advantage of the easy road access along the 100-foot-wide flow.

The tranquil nature of the stream ends as it flows down from the park above. Up there it becomes the usual beautifully stair-stepped mountainside fishery, offering deep holes among the boulders for native trout hideaways, plus rapids above the drop-offs which should be productive. The stream bottom has the pale glow peculiar to some freestone streams.

The Rose River is one of the better known Shenandoah Park streams, probably because of its size. There are approximately thirty open trout fisheries within the park boundaries, many quite small. "Approximately" applies because, depending upon drought or fish population, various smaller streams are closed at times. It is a good idea to check on conditions with the park information services, particularly during the summer. There are a total of ninety streams holding trout within the Shenandoah National Park. Native trout are the most precious and fragile resource within the preserve, and care is taken to prevent depletion.

AUTHOR'S NOTE: The Rose is a paradoxical stream. It's labeled a brook trout fishery and harbors some large specimens, but stories have filtered out of the Rose about big browns—eighteen inches or so—which are probably holdovers from stocked fish which have migrated upstream into native trout water. They are rare, but their foot-and-a-half-plus size has a way of jolting all preconceptions of brook trout fishing from your mind. The browns live here on borrowed time, since it is the policy of Shenandoah Park trout management to remove all but the native brook trout. Not everyone agrees with that policy. And although the few brown trout caught here are outsize, the wisdom of park management seems borne out by the disproportionately large heads of these browns, indicating inadequate food for such large specimens.

Another of the Rose's paradoxes is its occasional drought of any angling action, despite ideal water conditions and plenty of trout shapes plainly visible, followed a day later by the same brookies eagerly flashing at a nymph from their dark stations beneath the deeply undercut boulders. Such fickle behavior is one of the perverse reasons fly-fishers keep coming back to the Shenandoah's native trout fisheries year after year.

According to those who fish the Rose River frequently, caddis fly, mayfly and stonefly hatches keep the surface action going well into June. After that, on a good day, terrestrials, and particularly small beetles, do well. However, there are no guarantees.

Directions: From the Skyline Drive, the stream is reached from Fisher's Gap parking area and hiking down the Rose River Fire Road. The trail follows most of the river down to the lower park boundary.

From below it may be reached from VA(s) 670, which at Banco branches off primary state VA 231 north toward Criglersville. Route 670 ends at the lower end of Rose River Fire Road, which is blocked to vehicles above the park boundary. Parking here is at a premium, because of the many hikers' vehicles lining the road.

SMITH CREEK, ROCKINGHAM COUNTY

STREAM TYPE: Limestone • USGS Broadway • DeLorme 73

Smith Creek, in Rockingham County, is not to be confused with the famous Smith River brown trout fishery in Franklin County. The creek begins with Lacey Springs, boiling up among the cress and other aquatic plants. It comes from the same limestone-water action which carved Luray Caverns and many similar caves in the vicinity. Flowing north, the regulated stretch passes through 100 percent pastureland with a gentle gradient.

Most of the way the west bank has been cut away about six feet, allowing one to approach the water unseen at a crouch. The upper stretch is bordered with bittersweet and brier bushes with the uncanny ability to snare any backcast. Lower down the stream widens and there are cleared banks making for textbook casts.

The downstream portion is surrounded by active cattle pasturage, and the animals have their run of the stream. This plus the warmer water lower down makes the upstream portion the more active fishery. In fact, back in the seventies, the Inland Fisheries people branded Smith Creek "borderline" because of the higher water temperatures downstream. This has changed, perhaps because of the additional overhanging tree growth now shading the stream more completely.

For someone who grew up in western Virginia, Smith Creek brings to mind small-boy memories of farm streams usually called "branches" or "cricks." On a Sunday afternoon the farmer might rise out of his leather easy chair long enough to take a city kid down to the pasture. There with a birch pole and nightcrawler, batches of "hornyheads" would be agitated out of their sabbath rest. And occasionally there would be the thrill of color flashing when a brookie was hauled out from underneath a small waterfall. The farmer would hold the scarlet and silver fish for a moment, and then release it back into the crick to be caught another Sunday.

Smith Creek is a larger version of that childhood crick, with brown trout instead of brook, plus some decent rainbows. When asked what flies to use early in the year, Ken Puckett recommended Chironomid Midges, Numbers 20–22, presumably with a two-pound leader. Mr.

Puckett is the Trout Unlimited member largely responsible for advancing Smith Creek's trout management to its present state. The most productive area seems to be between the first and second fence crossings. Up near Lacey Springs some smaller rainbows actively feed among the clusters of aquatic plants. Farther downstream their larger relatives are occasionally hooked.

During warmer weather an Adams Number 18 can be an effective attractor. Later in the summer, when grasshoppers abound in the meadow, the Letort Hopper dry and Shenks Cricket dry are the most effective lures on the Smith as well as most Virginia spring creeks.

Smith Creek has the potential of becoming a good brown trout fishery, although it will probably never achieve the status of Mossy Creek because of its higher water temperature and use by cattle. The latter could change. As it stands, Smith Creek is an easy place to while away a warm spring afternoon in a most pleasant manner along with the browns and resident colony of Canada geese.

Special Regulations: Fly-fishing only, with conventional fly rod and single-hook artificial flies; no more than 18 feet of leader permitted, creel limit 2 fish per day; all fish less than 16 inches long must be handled carefully and returned unharmed to the water; possession of a fish less than 16 inches long on this water is illegal; possession of bait on this water is illegal; access must be at designated parking and fence-crossing points; wading, camping, and fires are prohibited; a signed landowner permit is required for fishing, obtainable from the Massanutten Chapter of Trout Unlimited or from Ken Puckett, 1138 Waterman Drive, Harrisonburg, Virginia 22801.

Directions: Take Exit 66 off I-81 to US 11 south. Go to Lacey Spring and turn east on VA(s) 806, then back north on VA(s) 986. Park at the gate.

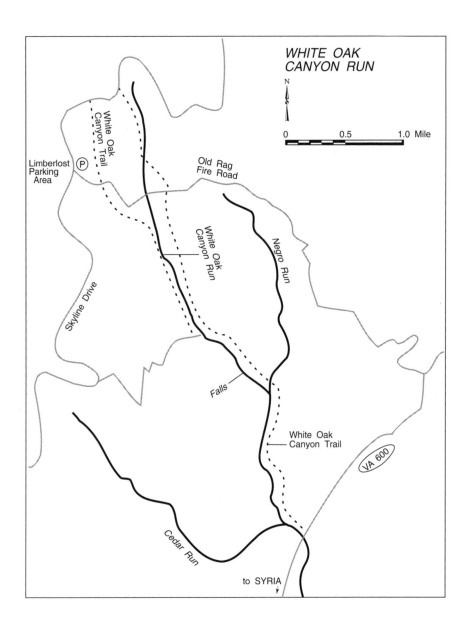

WHITE OAK
CANYON RUN

N

0   0.5   1.0 Mile

White Oak Canyon Trail

Limberlost Parking Area

(P)

Old Rag Fire Road

White Oak Canyon Run

Negro Run

Skyline Drive

Falls

White Oak Canyon Trail

VA 600

Cedar Run

to SYRIA

WHITE OAK CANYON RUN

STREAM TYPE: Freestone • USGS Old Rag Mountain
DeLorme 74

This is a stream of superlatives, and although everyone has his best trout water, White Oak Canyon Run is the favorite of more than a few. A visiting stream-lasher from Arizona or New Mexico, or even eastern Oregon, may be excused for his questioning of the so-called "poverty belt" of the Appalachians upon taking his first look at White Oak Canyon Run. For the westerner, these millions of gallons of cold, pure water from the Appalachian aquifer are a treasure precious as diamonds.

Although not the most productive Shenandoah Park stream, it may be enjoyed purely as a trout fishery, with no need to look further than the dazzling native trout, some of them reaching a foot and longer. Or the trout-seeker with a taste for entomology can occupy himself full time observing the frequent mayfly, caddis fly, and stonefly hatches. Hikers take the White Oak Canyon Trail purely for the beauty of the stream and the virgin hemlocks along its banks.

Before fishing here the first time, it's a good idea to walk in from above and see the stream's beginning, starting with fingers of water in a shining creep across the top of the ground. The fingers suddenly all converge with a roar into a fist, making a mature stream with holes ten feet deep or better. Next take a hike below the falls and look back up at the total volume reached. There is a bolt of white water roaring through an eighty-foot granite chute, falling to the valley floor below. Even the most intrepid French kayaker would be unable to make it through this chute in one piece—without a parachute. With a full appreciation of the stream's personality, you can fish it with an even more complete enjoyment.

Waders are a must here, as is a complete assortment of Number 16 or 18 dry flies and nymphs. Accessible as they are, the native brookies have a habit of coming up for a close look at your lure and then turning disdainfully away. Or what is even more disquieting, they strike the blood knot in your leader. This is a sure sign that a 6X or (seriously) 7X leader is what they prefer, tied to the smallest fly you can manage.

The usual tactics of staying low, using all available camouflage and cover, and going slow apply emphatically on this stream. Casual fishing will produce an abundance of near-fingerling-size brook trout, but the heavy hitters can only be enticed from their rock hideaways with extreme care and some skill.

One Blue Ridge Parkway-dwelling fisherman favors log-walking as a method of approaching the more canny larger fish without being spotted. There are huge hemlock logs frequently acting as bridges high above the channel. Easing out onto one of them and casting upstream will occasionally catch a hungry brookie by surprise.

Be prepared to make a day of it. And be prepared for dazzling surroundings. You'll be tempted to cast a fly into every enticing piece of tailwater along White Oak Canyon Run.

Directions: To avoid confusion, be aware that some old-timers still refer to White Oak Canyon Run as Robinson River. The most convenient park entry to this stream is from the Limberlost Parking Area on the east side of Skyline Drive at milepost 43. A tenth of a mile hike down Old Rag Fire Road leads to White Oak Canyon Trail. This clearly marked, gentle pathway takes you to the stream and continues all the way to the falls and the bottom of the mountain. To reach it from the bottom, you can drive in on VA(s) 600 to streamside and follow White Oak Canyon Trail up from there.

3

Allegheny Highlands

Bordered to the north by Highland County, this area is where the great eastern rivers, the Potomac and James, begin before any hint of pollution is felt. Highland County lists its population at around 3,000, fewer people than in the 1930s and only one fifth as many as the present sheep population. No such census of trout is available, but it is a safe bet that the rainbows outnumber the people here. Highland has the highest mean elevation east of the Mississippi, averaging heights of all the county's peaks. This explains why there was never a railroad through it and why the hardwood timber country has remained primarily an outdoor recreational paradise.

Just south of Highland is Bath County, where the Jackson River becomes one of the state's big water trout streams in Hidden Valley. Below Gathright Dam in Allegheny County, the lower Jackson is rapidly becoming one of the most talked-about trout fisheries in the state. Above the dam, Lake Moomaw is stocked regularly with brown and lake-run rainbow trout, along with a number of warm-water species. The shoreline is adjacent to the 13,428-acre T. M. Gathright Wildlife Management Area, under the supervision of the Virginia Department of Game and Inland Fisheries. Although all native game species are managed and produced here, the specialty is wild turkey.

Funded by the federal government, the Gathright Dam impound-ment serves a number of purposes, the most relevant being improve-

ment of water quality in the upper Jackson River by increasing its flow during periods of drought. The greater flow of cool water raises oxygen levels and washes away stagnant pools, creating ideal conditions for trout spawning and growth. An added plus for those launching a canoe at one of the six authorized ramps, the consistent water level has enhanced what was already a beautiful streamside vista.

This area generally contains the state's really big trout waters—the Jackson, Bullpasture and Maury rivers, for example. Here there is plenty of room for a big loop of backcast without snagging a limb. On the other hand a little bushwhacking can lead to some public lands containing very private smaller wild trout streams, such as Benson Run. The more adventurous take note: snagging a tough rhododendron leaf is the order of the day on these rugged little Allegheny Highlands waters.

BACK CREEK

STREAM TYPE: Primarily limestone, some freestone
USGS Mountain Grove, Sunrise • DeLorme 65

Back Creek is a sizable stream, by Virginia mountain standards, with deep rapids requiring chest waders for full coverage. Driving into the Blowing Springs campground area, you may park at the entrance to a road closed to vehicles, which puts you within easy walking distance to good fishing on Back Creek.

West of Blowing Springs, VA 39 parallels Back Creek upstream, with frequent gravel turnoffs. From these there are well-traveled paths leading down to the deeper holes. This is a signal that the less heavily fished areas are away from these beaten paths. What many do not realize is that the larger fish are lying in the rapids or small potholes between them.

Were it not next to a busy highway leading into West Virginia, complete with eighteen-wheelers, Back Creek might see fewer weekend anglers. In midweek, the traffic tends to die down, particularly as hot weather arrives in June. Downstream from Blowing Springs, the stream departs from the highway into an area called Back Creek Gorge, reached by a walking trail only. This eases the fishing pressure slightly. Farther down there seems to be a run of McGahey rainbows migrating up from Lake Moomaw, providing a special kind of fishing.

Near Blowing Springs is a gaging station operated by the Virginia Division of Water Resources. The information recorded there is used to measure the amount of water drained from Back Creek's 131 square miles of watershed. During one decade the recorded maximum flow was 65,450 gallons per second. Above the gaging station the stream is crossed by a concrete bridge, where the sign indicates Big Back Creek. The old bridge abutment still remains, and where it projects into the stream is a likely hideout for a big brown or two. Just past the

The author, on a regulated stretch of Back Creek.

bridge posted land begins and continues to the village of Mountain Grove, where Little Back Creek merges with the main stream.

The headwaters hold brook and rainbow, while downstream is dominated by browns and rainbow. Brook trout are more prevalent north of the Highland–Bath county line. There are excellent spring mayfly hatches all along the stream, including Quill Gordon and March Browns. Winter stoneflies are present into early spring. The most consistently effective attractor fly is the Adams Number 14 or 16, along with Wulffs and hair wings.

Upstream of Mountain Grove is a short stretch of regulated fishing, single-hook, artificial lures, with a limit of two trout over sixteen inches. These waters are maintained by the Virginia Electric Power Company as part of their Bath County Pumped Storage Station Recreation Area. Be prepared for a stream which looks a little as though it might have been designed by the Corps of Engineers, with chiseled stone ripraps forming the banks.

Directions: Turn west off US 220 onto VA 39 west. Cross Back Creek Mountain into the George Washington National Forest. Turn left at the sign reading "Blowing Springs Campground."

To reach the special-regulations stretch, turn left from VA 39 onto VA(s) 600 at Hiner's store and proceed south to the Recreation Area entrance.

BENSON RUN

STREAM TYPE: Freestone • USGS Deerfield • DeLorme 65

If there were a T-shirt reading, "I Rode the Road to Benson Run—and Survived," it could be worn with pride by a very special cadre of trout fishermen. When you mention this stream to the older generation of hardy anglers, their eyes glaze over as they say things like, "Yeah, I was up there in 'fifty-one. Lost my exhaust pipe on that @#!!! road."

As you enter the road to Benson Run, you will see the U.S. Department of Agriculture sign with the word "gate" chiseled in the wood and hung on—you guessed it—a gate. Farther up the mountain there is the usual yellow diamond sign reading "Rough Road." If there ever were an award for understatement, this sign would win without question. The single-lane road climbs abruptly, and then swings down off the mountain into a flood plain. Here is where the springs of your vehicle, along with your tailbone, get a thumping from the potholes.

Occasionally it is necessary to dodge around a fresh-cut tree stump in the middle of the road. Attempting to ride above the ruts, you slide into them frequently because there's no shoulder. Then there is a six-foot dropoff where floods have taken out a section of the road. At this point it becomes necessary to strike out through the woods between trees far enough apart to accommodate both fenders. After about an hour of this, most of it at five miles per hour, Benson Run begins to look more and more fishable, and it's time to find a space wide enough to park your four-wheel-drive. (Don't drive to Benson Run in anything less!)

Approaching the stream, you are impressed most by the cathedral-like quality of the huge hemlocks on the flood plain, which let slices of sunlight through. The quiet is absolute, except for the sighing of the stream and perhaps a pileated woodpecker at work. Situated on a mountain plateau, Benson Run is not one of the boisterous, roaring spring streams usually found in this area. It flows beyond a number of alternate beds, now dry, cut by Hurricane Hugo in 1989. The banks are around four feet high and closely held by hemlock and pine trees. Casting a fly requires some patience, and it helps to take a deep breath and a careful look at the network of limbs above a pool before making the first cast to it.

There are a couple of requirements for the trip to Benson Run. First, have a four-wheel-drive vehicle in good condition. If it fails on you at the end of the road, there's quite a hike out to get help. Second, be prepared to bounce arrhythmically, as there's no pattern to the potholes and rocks in the roadway to Benson Run. And lastly, be assured that the trip will be worthwhile. There's so little adventure left in the lower eastern U.S. that sometimes it goes unrecognized or is mistaken for discomfort and inconvenience. There's plenty of both on the trip up to Benson Run, but there's a biting edge of adventure about it as well.

Directions: Williamsville, unlike Williamsburg, is not a readily recognized Virginia landmark, consisting as it does of a post office, abandoned store, and not much else. From VA 39 just west of Millboro Springs, look for the sign where VA(s) 678 turns north. Follow it to the outskirts of Williamsville, where the road forks right to a concrete bridge across the Cowpasture River. This is VA(s) 614, which becomes a gravel road just past the firehouse. Follow 614 a couple of miles to a high cut in the road looking down on the confluence of Benson Run with the Cowpasture. Down at the bottom of the cut there is a farmhouse which has been converted into the Benson Run Hunt Club. Turn in there and look for the gate, which you should close behind you. Ford the stream, and begin the stretch of rugged roadway which takes you to some fine brook trout fishing.

For the less adventurous, there are two additional access routes. One is FR 173, which turns to the west off of VA(s) 629 approximately two miles north of the town of Deerfield. The other is a spur off of FR 394, known as the Sugar Tree Road. This is reached by following VA(s) 614 as above, turning to the right at the Sugar Tree sign a couple of miles before reaching Benson Run and driving up the mountain to a spur on the left designated FR 394B. From the dead end it's a short hike to the fishing area.

BUFFALO CREEK

STREAM TYPE: Limestone • USGS Glasgow • DeLorme 53

Approaching very carefully the deep pool just above the footbridge at the downstream end of the special regulation section may give you your first clue to what kind of trout stream the Buffalo is. Often there are brown trout lying next to the bank ranging in length from eighteen to twenty-four inches. If you are fortunate enough to spot these giants, it won't be for long. They soon disappear to parts unknown and are very fickle about coming out to take flies. This same stretch is the scene of much frenzied surface feeding.

From the footbridge at the only parking area to a sign downstream reading "Trout Sanctuary" there is no fishing allowed. The Buffalo describes an 180-degree loop about the landowner's home, and he has courteously requested that the loop be designated a sanctuary to protect his privacy. So although no real fish-management purpose is served by the sanctuary, it shelters a permanently undisturbed population of trout.

Buffalo Creek is formed by the confluence of two limestone spring streams and is fed along the way by numerous other smaller springs, guaranteeing a good summer flow. Along its low to moderate gradient are several textbook pools and many large, deep flats. Below the sanctuary the last mile of regulated stream cuts through a gorge dominated by large boulders and bedrock ledges. The footing is more slippery in the gorge, and additional care should be used when wading.

The usual hatches in this area can be imitated by a Ginger Quill Number 14, Adams 16, Light Cahill 16, or Dark Hendrickson 14. When all else fails, small terrestrials such as black and cinnamon ants may be productive.

Just about any time of day you can see surface activity, but don't be misled. Despite all the pops and splashes, these fish give new meaning to the word "wary." They have seen more fly and leader combinations than Rat-Faced MacDougal, and will continue to feed inches away from your Light Cahill or Ginger Quill deceivers.

Another challenge on the Buffalo is the thick overhang of young maples, sycamores, and alders. These require most casts to be made from midstream, and even there it helps to roll-cast frequently. In other words, Buffalo Creek is a stream which truly tests your fly-fishing ability. You may do everything right, stalking the two-footers from downstream, making a perfect cast, laying out your hatch-match just above their noses, double-hauling what little slack may have been left from your feather-light drop. And with all that, you may finish a day on the Buffalo with pleasant memories of everything except that line-parting tug which only a citation brown can give.

Special Regulations: Fishing restricted to single-hook artificial lures; creel limit 2 fish per day; all trout less than 16 inches long must be handled carefully and returned unharmed to the water; possession of trout less than 16 inches long on this water is illegal; trespassing in areas marked as fish sanctuaries is illegal; camping, alcoholic beverages, firearms, swimming, fires and picnicking are prohibited; wading is permitted; access must be at designated parking and fence-crossing points. Written permission to fish is needed, as this water is private property; the landowner's rights must be respected, and failure to do so may result in loss of fishing privileges. Permission slips may be obtained at a Virginia Game and Inland Fisheries office or from the landowner's home at streamside.

Directions: Take VA 251 west off of 11, just south of Lexington. Follow 251 to VA(s) 612 and turn south. Route 612 follows the stream in a southerly direction, and offers one designated parking area and a number of other places where you can pull off the road, adjacent to some of the best fishing stretches.

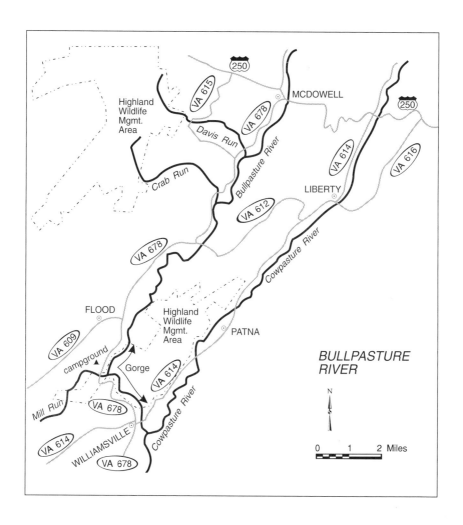

BULLPASTURE
RIVER

BULLPASTURE RIVER

STREAM TYPE: Limestone • USGS Monterey, Williamsville
DeLorme 65

The name of this river, Bullpasture, and its course, flowing into the
Cowpasture, conjures a quiet, flat stream meandering through
pastureland. Nothing could be further from the truth along the 5½
miles of public trout water. This spectacular stream rises in Highland

County, where the sheep population far outnumbers the human. It was named by early settlers for the numerous eastern buffalo which watered there, wearing deep trails which are moss-covered but still visible along the bank two centuries later.

The upper stretch is mostly privately owned, posted against fishing, and indeed does run through comparatively flat cattle-grazing land for a short distance. Then a few miles above Williamsville, the Bullpasture takes a sudden drop through a rugged, wooded canyon called "the gorge." Looking remarkably like a western river, it tumbles against cabin-size boulders, forming deep pools which hold trout throughout the summer months. Frequent cold springs feed into this gorge sector, giving the water an icy freshness even in July and August. Maintained by the State Game Commission, the gorge area fills the eye with hemlocks marching a thousand feet down the side of Bullpasture Mountain plus a parade of wildlife to distract one's concentration from a drifting Adams or Cahill.

Deer, wild turkeys, mink, wildcats, and otters may cause some of the shadows moving along the bank. But don't expect all to be pristine wilderness. The Bullpasture is stocked water, and has been one of Virginia's most successful put-and-take streams since the state's trout-stocking program began. Rainbow, brown, and brook trout are provided regularly, and an attempt was even made at one time to start a population of Bitterroot browns, which failed. It was theorized that the six-inch Bitterroot fingerlings were outcompeted by the larger fish population already in place.

Above the gorge a small spring creek called Mill Run empties in, and at its mouth there is a public campground which tends to be crowded during the peak trout season. Called by some the number-one Virginia trout stream, the Bullpasture is well publicized and tends to be heavily populated with spin fishermen. One way to get away from a weekend crowd is to explore the many spring creeks, such as Mill Run and Davis Run, in the vicinity of the Bullpasture. These creeks hold small but lively wild rainbows which must be stalked carefully and then tempted with a fly dangled three or four feet from your rod tip.

Finding these little gems may take some exploring, and you can be sure no self-respecting native trout angler will tell you about his favorite spring creek. But the effort of searching is well worth it. One should not be dismayed at the number of spin casters and other

Netting a brown on one of the rare placid stretches of the Bullpasture.

competitors. The wilier fish, particularly browns, have plenty of room to elude them in the average twenty-five-foot width of the Bullpasture, and there are multitudes of deep hiding holes beneath the rocks where a nymph or Muddler Minnow can be dangled with good success.

Another way of escaping the crowd is winter fishing the Bullpasture, at the risk of taking a header into three feet of pure, ice-rimmed misery. Even in January trout are active in Virginia, and some nice holdover fish may be taken. Because of the water volume of the Bullpasture, wilier fish elude the fair-weather anglers. The Virginia trout season lasts until February, but it doesn't hurt to have a white oak fire crackling in a nearby fireplace when wading at near-freezing air temperatures.

During any season the key to choosing the right fly for the Bullpasture is versatility. Be prepared with a good assortment of dry flies, plus some wets and nymphs for the many rapids and holes beneath small waterfalls. An all-round good choice is the Adams Number 16, but it's advisable to check the Bullpasture hatches, as they change frequently. Sampling the duns can give a clue to those whirls of activity just under the surface. An opaque, flush-floating terrestrial such as a flying ant, gypsy moth or jassid may do the trick in late spring or summer. Sometimes you may spot green inchworms dropping from the many overhanging limbs, and adding an artificial greenie is sure to stir up the hungry mayhem.

One of the less encouraging sights in the Bullpasture are flashes of silver from the bellies of fish working the bottom. Examining the stomach contents of a brown deep-hooked amid such activity may reveal a handful of small black snail shells, for which there is no artificial counterpart. But the amateur entomologist should be prepared for such myriad invertebrate surprises brimming over in this exciting stream, and go with the flow.

Directions: The Bullpasture River is virtually 100 percent accessible by vehicle from VA(s) 678 all the way to Williamsville. Deep in the gorge are some stretches which demand a little extra legwork, and consequently aren't as heavily fished as the roadside holes. One such example is a series of parallel rock shelves which stretch between steep banks. The troughs between these shelves are deep enough to make chest waders a must, but can usually be relied upon for trout action any time of the year.

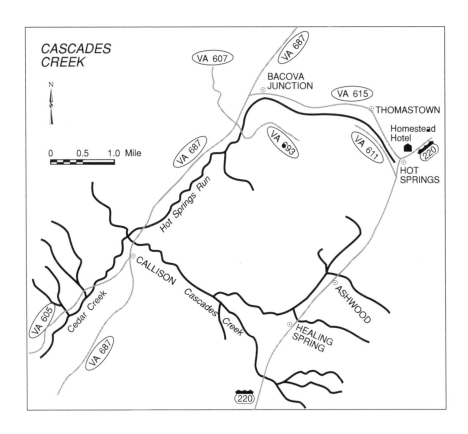

THE CASCADES CREEK

STREAM TYPE: Limestone • USGS Healing Springs • DeLorme 52

As you descend from the Homestead's Cascades Inn down a gravel road to the stream, the altitude drops more than 800 feet. It becomes obvious that this is a different sort of environment altogether from that of the high ground. There is a celebration of life in this water-rich gorge, both animal and plant. The stream is surrounded by around 16,000 acres of private land, much of it virgin forest.

On the rock cliff above the stream there are jack-in-the-pulpits with overleafs the size of small girl's hand. Rare blood-red trillium abound, along with wild orchids and scarlet columbine. One has the feeling that

Beaver Shriver, Cascades guide and proprietor of "The Outpost" fly shop, fishing his home stream.

there must be some brilliantly colored rainbows beneath the surface of these pools to match all this glory above, and that is truly the case.

The three-mile stretch of privately stocked and maintained stream is the private domain of Beaver Shriver, who acts as guide for those lucky enough to discover the Cascades. He can identify the ten or twelve varieties of nymphs revealed on an overturned stone, and hand you his "secret weapon," a Light Cahill spinner fly he tied that morning. He can then introduce you to the hefty rainbow waiting just where he knows it will be, ready to smash his spinner. Afterward Beaver can demonstrate his technique of using forceps to remove the hook, releasing the trout without touching it.

You have your choice of a guided or solo trip. The experienced fly-fisherman may wish to explore the Cascades on his own, starting at the downstream end where there are startlingly clear pools for sharp-shooting at rises with dry flies. Moving up, one encounters the falls that give the stream its name. These are unstocked waters, with wild rainbows in the lees and eddies beneath frequent waterfalls. It takes a little hand-over-handing over stone cliffs to reach the pools, but the effort is worth it. Where the stone has been pounded by falling water for several millennia, the plunge pools are deep, as may be expected. Here a weighted nymph or Muddler is appropriate, despite Beaver's persuasion as a dry-fly purist.

In the Homestead tradition, novice fly-fishers will be treated with the same courtesy and respect as seasoned stream-lashers. The fishing pro, either Beaver Shriver or one of his assistants, is available at the Cascades Inn at 8:00 to 9:00 A.M. and 1:00 to 2:00 P.M. daily. After that he may be reached at the stream. For early morning fishing, it is advisable to make arrangements the night before. Fly-fishing lessons are conducted on the stream for first-timers or seasoned anglers who wish to polish their technique.

Rods, reels and lines are for rent at the Cascades Inn, and flies and accessories are for sale. The permit to fish is $20 per day for Homestead guests and Trout Unlimited members, $24 for all others.

Fishermen must have a Virginia state fishing license or trip-fishing license, valid for five successive days. State residents pay $5.50 for trip licenses, while nonresidents are charged $6.50. All licenses are available at the Cascades Inn. The private permit specifies that only fishing with flies is authorized. Many prefer to release all fish, but in some cases Homestead guests turn their catches over to the hotel chef for presentation at dinner that evening.

The Cascades experience may not be for everyone, but there is nothing artificial about it. In no way does it resemble fishing a manicured English meadow stream. On the contrary it is wilder and relatively more untouched than most other Virginia trout waters.

Directions: Drive Rt. 220 north to the Homestead Hotel at Hot Springs and ask for Mr. Beaver Shriver, trout-fishing specialist, at the Outpost Cottage Store. For advance information, call (703) 839-5355 or (703) 839-5442.

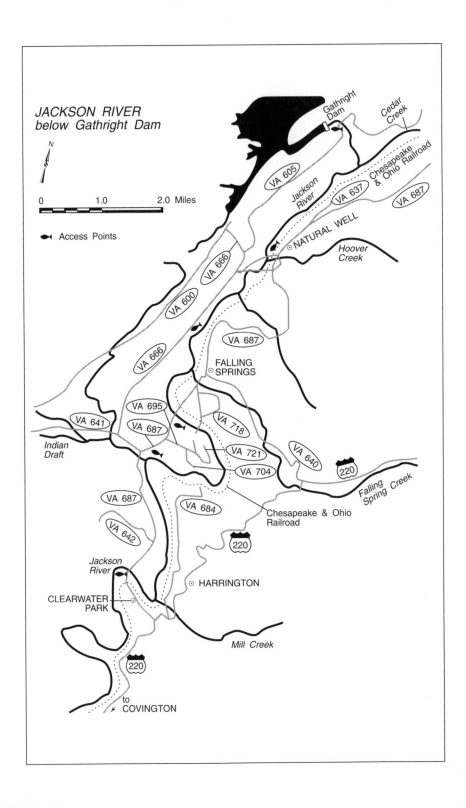

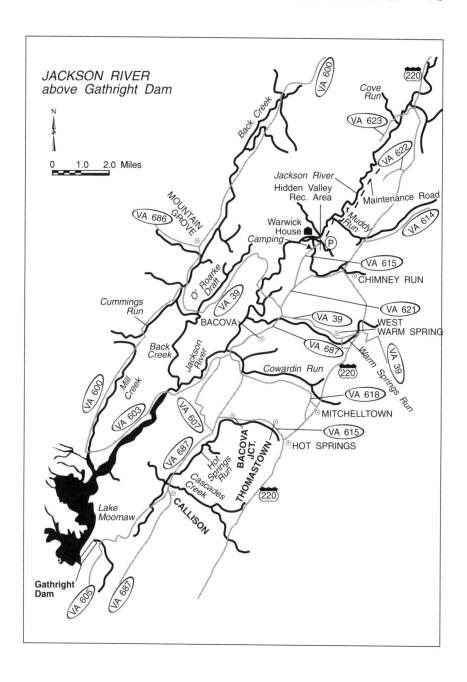

JACKSON RIVER
above Gathright Dam

N

0   1.0   2.0 Miles

VA 600

Cove
Run

VA 623

VA 622

Back Creek

Jackson River
Hidden Valley
Rec. Area

Maintenance Road

MOUNTAIN
GROVE

VA 686

Warwick
House
Camping

Muddy
Run

P

VA 614

VA 615

CHIMNEY RUN

O' Roarke
Draft

Cummings
Run

VA 39

VA 621

VA 39

WEST
WARM SPRING

BACOVA

VA 687

VA 39

Back
Creek

Jackson
River

Cowardin Run

Warm Springs Run

220

VA 600

Mill
Creek

VA 618

MITCHELLTOWN

VA 603

VA 607

VA 615

HOT SPRINGS

VA 687

Hot
Springs
Run

BACOVA
JCT.

THOMASTOWN

220

Cascades
Creek

Lake
Moomaw

CALLISON

Gathright
Dam

VA 605

VA 687

JACKSON RIVER

STREAM TYPE: Limestone • USGS Warm Springs, Falling Spring
DeLORME 64, 65

The Jackson is one of western Virginia's primary waterways, and this chapter concentrates upon only one small section of it, the Hidden Valley Recreation Area. It should be noted that a stretch of the Jackson below Gathright Dam is under development as a stock-and-grow project. At present it is fished by boat, with parties putting in just below the dam and drifting. The catch-and-release program there is flourishing, and this stretch of the Jackson has the potential of being one of the state's premier trout waters in the near future.

For trout fishermen who need relief from the precious gemlike cascades and grottoes of Virginia's small mountain streams, the Jackson is relatively big water, at least in western Virginia terms. It is around 100 feet across at Hidden Valley, and at times much wider. There are riffles punctuated by long stretches of quiet water ideal for dry-fly-fishing. Beginning in late April, fish may be seen rising there nearly every evening. There is excellent holdover brown fishing throughout Hidden Valley. And even though the Jackson does not have the immensity of some trout streams in Wyoming, say, or New Hampshire, or even Pennsylvania, none of those states has Virginia bluebells growing upon their stream banks in May.

To the first-time fisher of Hidden Valley, the most striking sight is the Warwick House across the river. It is a pre–Civil War mansion with its four massive Ionic columns still intact after nearly two centuries. This imposing dwelling could very well have been the home of Scarlett O'Hara's Virginia cousins, though appropriately enough it is now being remodeled as a bed-and-breakfast catering to trout anglers.

Even further back in the history of this area, George Washington inspected the forts along the Jackson in 1755. It's tempting to speculate that the young George took time to cut a hickory sapling and try his luck with the native brook trout with which the stream was packed during that century.

To fish the most productive site along the Jackson River, one must first walk about three miles up a maintenance road on which no motorized traffic is allowed. Although this does not seem a long distance, the road is scattered with heel-less athletic socks eaten away by the chafing of waders. The combination of waders, socks, and three miles of road, level though it is, can be destructive. One ingenious father and his young son were observed riding bicycles with fly rods strapped to their handlebars. This was one solution to the distance problem. Another would be to shoulder your waders and wear a good pair of walking shoes as far as the swinging bridge.

As part of the Jackson River fishing experience, Muddy Run is worth including. Upstream almost to the swinging bridge, this small stream flows into the Jackson from the east. It is not muddy at all, but has a perpetually milky appearance from the mineral content of the soil through which it flows. A hefty population of wild rainbows can be roused from beneath its banks with a streamer or timely nymph. There is a marked trail following Muddy Run upstream until posted property is reached. It's a good sidebar trip away from the Jackson if the river trout aren't biting, or if your addictions tend toward Virginia's string of smaller watery gems gracing the state's western mountains.

Directions: From US 220 turn west on VA 39, go about 3 miles to VA(s) 621, and turn north on 621 to the Hidden Valley Recreation Area. Follow VA(s) 621 for about a mile and then turn left onto VA(s) 615. After 1½ miles, you will reach the Hidden Valley Recreation Area. There is a camping section to the left with well-manicured facilities and a parking area straight ahead.

JERRY'S RUN

STREAM TYPE: Freestone • USGS Jerry's Run • DeLorme 52

Jerry's Run is one of Virginia's highly visible streams which manages to retain its identity despite notoriety. The angler-athlete should be prepared to hike in to the most desirable native trout stretch, as the stream diverges right, away from the road. The only access from that point is a short, rutty road leading to a walking trail along the stream, which becomes very dim in spots but continues for around four miles.

At the National Forest boundary Jerry's Run flows into a fair-sized pond, which marks the end of trout fishing. There is no access from below, as below the pond the land belongs to the CSX Railroad, with emphatic No Trespassing signs posted about.

There are enough feeder streams to maintain fishing through a dry September, and it's an ideal location for trying small autumn terrestrials. You will more than likely have the stream to yourself at this season. This may be due to both a lack of autumn stocking of Jerry's Run and the opening of bow-hunting season occupying outdoor sportsmen around the same time.

Jerry's Run is a slate-bottom stream with a gentle gradient throughout its length, with consequently only a few really deep holes. From the cut bank around six feet high you can look into the glass-clear shallows and spot a few decent-sized rainbows. Once located, these heavy-bodied fish can be stalked carefully from downstream. There's a lack of aquatic insects, apparently, with an abundance of small minnows. Some surface feeding has been spotted, but its objectives were too small for recognition—probably gnats or similar small terrestrials.

The upstream stretch is five minutes away from the Interstate exit bearing its name, so as might be expected, you won't immediately find the darting native trout shapes there which are apparent in the less convenient Appalachian streams. Farther downstream, where there is a four-mile stretch with no vehicle access, the brook trout are more numerous in direct proportion to the lack of discarded beverage cans.

The surrounding national forest land has been timbered over within the last fifteen years, so there are streamside clearings with enough backcasting room to place a fly from some distance away. This is a necessity because of the clarity of this shallow water, and because these are rod-wise fish who flee at the first sign of movement.

At one point there is a feeder stream flowing beneath the road and into a ten-foot-deep hole. There are signs of strenuous stream management here, with stones encased in woven wire and partial dams. The hole is probably heavily stocked, and just as heavily harvested by fishermen who can step from their vehicles and cast into the pool. This is typical of the upper stretch, and fly-fishermen looking for natives should continue downstream until the path is less clearly trampled down.

Directions: From I-64 headed west from Covington, take the Jerry's Run Trail exit, almost to the West Virginia line. Turn left at the stop sign onto FR 198, which immediately becomes a single-lane, unpaved two-track. The road parallels Jerry's Run downstream, where it becomes FR 69. Where it diverges left up Brushy Mountain, there is a dirt lane leading right, with the usual understated "Rough Road" sign.

MAURY RIVER

STREAM TYPE: Freestone • USGS Goshen • DeLorme 53

On VA 39 between Goshen and Interstate 81, the area called Goshen Pass is one of the most breathtaking bits of scenic beauty in Virginia. The Maury River is another roadside stream, but there's enough of it to accommodate a fair crowd of cruising fishermen. It requires some patience with one's fellow man to fish here, as it's likely to be dredged out by bait fishermen shortly after stocking earlier in the season. But the Maury is one of those streams which might be worth a visit in June, since the proximity of good bass fishing nearby, indeed on the lower reaches of the Maury itself, may filter out some competition.

Higher up, at an area called Devil's Kitchen, there are stretches of class 3, 4, and 5 whitewater canoeing, some of Virginia's best. As you might gather, it is advisable to wear chest waders here, and to step forward with care in these rapids. Farther down, below the white water, there are some wide pools with plenty of cleared space for backcasting, an ideal location for sharpshooting at rising fish with Light Cahills or Hendricksons. Around dusk, or even just after, a large white moth may coax some lure-wise brown from its favorite boulder.

Directions: From I-81 take East Lexington Exit 53 west on VA 39. Follow it to the Goshen Pass scenic area through which the Maury River flows.

MILL CREEK

STREAM TYPE: Limestone • USGS Millboro • DeLORME 53, 65

Any trout enthusiast driving down VA 39 toward Goshen Pass will be distracted by the inviting stretch of Mill Creek paralleling the highway. This is a busy two-lane road, with little room to pull off onto the shoulder. Nevertheless, there is good trout water along VA 39 for several miles before the road reaches the town of Goshen. And even there, behind the Mill Creek Cafe, the water looks fishable.

Best results may be had along that portion of Mill Creek beginning at the Rockbridge/Bath County line, where moderately impressive boulders cause the water to pause and cascade down into deep holes. Like many active Virginia mountain streams, the Mill is conducive to fishing wet rather than dry. A dry fly has a hard time staying above water among the heavy riffles and falls. But as the prominent trout author E. R. Hewitt said back in the thirties, 80 percent of a trout's diet consists of underwater life forms, 30 percent nymphs plus others.

Woolly Worms do particularly well in the heavy water of Mill Creek when cast upstream into cascading water and allowed to run into the depths beneath. If that's not working, switching to Muddlers or other minnow-imitation streamers might stir up the trout population.

One of the burdens of Appalachian fishermen is parting the rhododendrons up some mountain draw and seeing four fishermen, one at each corner of a choice pool. This will not happen on Mill Creek. It's a "drive-in" stream, and that is both a blessing and a curse. On the positive side, it may be cruised from VA 39 to spot the most inviting and least populated waters. On the negative, being so public, it can have multiple vehicles parked above its choice pools, particularly on weekends early in the season. Later on, when the mayflies become thicker and fishermen thin out, there's more elbow room on this stream, which incidentally has enough miles of fishing water to absorb a goodly number of bug-watchers.

Directions: From I-81 take the East Lexington Exit 53 west on VA 39. Follow it through the town of Goshen, above which Mill Creek parallels 39.

Mossy Creek is considered to be the state's number one trout stream by many Virginia fly fishers.

MOSSY CREEK

STREAM TYPE: Limestone • USGS Parnassus • DeLorme 66

At the south shank of the Shenandoah Valley is the stream considered number one for trout by many informed Virginia fly-fishers. Certainly during late summer and early fall, when hoppers are falling into the stream, the Mossy's big browns will explode onto imitation cricket or grasshopper lures. Regardless of the unwinnable debate over which is first in Virginia's family of trout streams, Mossy Creek ranks high. And it makes an ideal first stop for someone beginning his exploration of western Virginia's trout habitat. It's also a good test area for the neophyte fly-caster, as its gentle, riffled pools and grassy banks are free of the usual laurel or hemlock branches grabbing for unwary fly hooks.

Thanks to constant caretaking by Trout Unlimited, Mossy is a "tame" stream, carefully manicured, flowing through pastureland reminiscent of famous limestone streams of central Pennsylvania with their whopping big brown trout. Turnstiles make cattle fences easy to negotiate without damage to the landowner's strands. There are no cans or polystyrene boxes littering the banks, the immaculate appearance of the area in general speaking well of the careful fishermen-landowner relationship which exists here.

Mossy Creek originates at a large limestone spring in the old mill pond at Mount Solon. The fishable section flows for a little over seven miles through private grazing land, with access only at designated parking sites and fence crossings. At present only three miles are open to public fishing.

Despite its name, the streambed contains no true moss, but rather a proliferation of rooted aquatic plants. Fishing wet flies produces occasional "hangs," which are easily freed up by snapping off a succulent watercress stem. Large springs feed in at frequent intervals, keeping the water at stable temperatures during the summer.

An active brown trout fingerling-stocking program was started on Mossy Creek in 1976 and is constantly under expansion. In 1989 electrofishing of seventy-two browns produced twenty-four fish between twelve and sixteen inches, and six rod-benders greater than sixteen inches in length. The Mossy also contains a few smallmouth and rock bass, but they have difficulty surviving the voracious big browns' appetites. Due to careful stream management, there is a sizable population of holdovers, supplemented by annual stockings of five to six-inch fingerlings.

The stream averages fifteen feet in width, with pools over twenty feet wide at most. Such close quarters makes for a little difficulty casting and working flies with a good drift. Delicate ties of standard dry patterns work best on the lure-wise trout in this stream's flat water.

During the prime hatching season, patterns for Mossy and most of

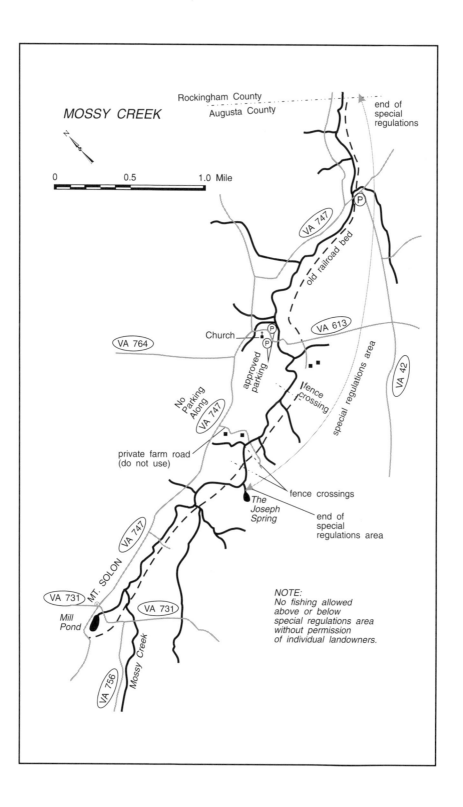

MOSSY CREEK

0   0.5   1.0 Mile

Rockingham County
Augusta County

end of
special
regulations

VA 747

old railroad bed

VA 613

Church

VA 764

approved parking

No Parking Along VA 747

VA 747

fence crossing

special regulations area

VA 42

private farm road
(do not use)

fence crossings

The Joseph Spring

end of
special
regulations area

VA 747

MT. SOLON

VA 731

VA 731

Mill Pond

NOTE:
No fishing allowed
above or below
special regulations area
without permission
of individual landowners.

VA 756

Mossy Creek

Virginia's other trout waters can be covered by old standby dry flies such as Ginger Quill, Adams, Light Cahill, Trico and Coachman patterns. During the gentle Virginia autumn and winter, terrestrial drys can be effective through most of the season, with year-round hatches. At the beginning of the hopper season a smaller, less obvious pattern such as the Letort Number 16 is preferred. During the crisper months it is helpful to have a good supply of such terrestrials as black flying ants and the Crowe Beetle Dry.

Unlike typical put-and-take streams, the Mossy is open twelve months of the year. On a warm day in February, when the first bloodroot sprouts begin pushing through, this is a fine place to take out that primal spring urge to wet a fly. Despite a slight milky color of the water this time of year, some smaller trout are very receptive to wets such as weighted Number 12 Muddlers and Pheasant Tail nymphs. A big black Wooly Bugger may tempt a larger brown to lash out of its winter sulk beneath the bank.

Make no mistake, Mossy Creek is not typical of Virginia's trout streams, which for the most part are boisterous mountain rapids with plunge pools formed by the boulders below. Nevertheless, it is a privilege to fish the manicured Mossy because of the obvious care which has been taken to keep this a prime trout fishery. For someone just entering the world of Virginia fly-fishing, this is an ideal location, with clear space for backcasts and an abundance of flat water furnishing predictable action throughout the year. A model of stream management, Mossy Creek affords a glimpse at the ideal, healthier future in store for Virginia's already flourishing trout program.

Special Regulations: Fishing restricted to single-hook artificial flies; creel limit 2 fish per day; all fish less than 16 inches long must be handled carefully and returned unharmed to the water; possession of fish less than 16 inches long on this water is illegal; possession of bait on this water is illegal; fishing permitted year round; access must be at designated parking and fence-crossing points; wading, camping and fires are prohibited. Written permission to fish is needed, as this water is private property; the landowner's rights must be respected, and failure to do so may result in loss of fishing privileges. Permission slips may be obtained at the Virginia Game and Inland Fisheries office in Staunton.

Directions: Take the Weyer's Cave exit east off of I-81. Go north on US 11 and turn west onto VA(s) 646. Turn south onto VA 42, and proceed to VA(s) 613, which is a gravel road. Turn west on 613, and proceed to marked parking areas.

THE POTOMAC RIVER

STREAM TYPE: Limestone • USGS Monterey • DeLorme 65

This is not the Potomac of Washington Tidal Basin fame, but rather the headwaters of the big river. Here George Washington could have flipped a tuppence across the Potomac with no strain to his presidential thumb. A bureaucrat originally anchored in Highland County derived some satisfaction driving to downtown D.C. each morning, looking at the Potomac's broad expanse and remembering its humble spring-fed origin.

Turning left just before US 220 reaches the West Virginia border, you follow the Potomac upstream 4.6 miles, all of which is stocked by the state with trout. At first there is a short stretch running through woods, but above that the river is totally surrounded by livestock pasturage—sheep in one field, cattle in another. You may assume from that that the Potomac will never be classic trout water, and you're probably correct. But if you're fishing other streams in the locality, such as the Jackson and Bullpasture rivers or Back Creek, the Potomac is worth a side trip. After all, how many people can say they caught a trout from the Potomac?

Because it's a meadow stream for the most part, a visit there will involve looking down from the road to a shining bronze ribbon cutting through green pasture. Then as one enters the village of Blue Grass on VA 642, a conspicuous sign by the road reads, "Caution—New Traffic Pattern." This turns out to be Blue Grass's new, and only, stop sign erected in the middle of town. Then the Potomac continues upstream through one livestock ranch after another. One wonders how the state stocking officials get through those hundred of yards of grazing land to deposit their trout in the Potomac.

Just upstream from Blue Grass there is a dam and the vestige of a mill. The series of cascades descending below the dam offer some promise to the wet-fly-caster. Even though the mill is in the village of Crab Bottom, the waters below it include some excellent trout habitat.

One could spend a day on the Potomac exploring the fishing possibilities, but also just enjoying the mountain-meadow scenery, reminiscent of Switzerland. Occasional flights of goldfinches swoop across the stream, so swift and brilliant against the green fields that it's hard to believe they were ever there. The relatively gentle mountains rise slowly on either side, level enough to support the prosperous ranches. The mountaintops are a reminder that Highland County has the greatest average altitude of any county east of the Mississippi.

Directions: Follow US 220 north out of Monterey, the seat of Highland County. Pass the Virginia Trout Hatchery to the right, and continue north to VA(s) 642, where a left turn puts you alongside the newborn Potomac.

POUNDING MILL CREEK

STREAM TYPE: Freestone • USGS Covington • DeLorme 52

The lower section of Pounding Mill Creek is posted by private landowners who have actually fenced it off. Where the pavement ends there is a sign indicating that FR 125 is a single-lane road with turnouts for passing. Here you come across the first sign nailed to a sycamore tree proclaiming trout-stocked waters. It is somewhat encouraging to note that the local service station operators a few blocks away are unaware of how to reach Pounding Mill via Dolly Ann Drive. The road is worth finding, however, as the drive through to Clifton Forge is a rarely experienced flight across high mountaintops, with sheer drop-offs and roadsides shot through with the color of cardinal flowers, yellow-eyed susans, and Dutchman's breeches during the summer.

Pounding Mill Creek is a good stream to avoid during hot summer months, when it becomes little more than a rivulet, about the width of a forearm's length. Even with the spring rains, this is a small stream, really small, making the uninformed fly-fisherman ask himself, "What am I doing here?" The answer lies in the many stocked and wild rainbows and wild brook trout scurrying for safety. For its size, this stream has a healthy and lively fish population, few if any of them citation size, but many quite ready to try the patience of a camouflage-clad stalker throughout a morning. If you're not a connoisseur of small crystalline watercourses trickling through heavy rhododendrons, then avoid Pounding Mill.

It's a gravel-bed stream with sizable enough boulders to afford shelter for trout. There has been some streambed management here, with granite ripraps at the lower section. Various hurricanes have molded this section of the stream into islands and small dams which have probably improved the habitat. Farther upstream where the hemlock overgrowth becomes heavier, there are nervous native trout darting away at alarming speed. Terrestrials are indicated here, with red and black ants recommended, along with hoppers during the summer.

Despite the lack of any water of appreciable depth upstream, there are logs placed across the stream by conservators, half-sawed in the center to form miniature waterfalls. From twenty yards away you can see a swarm of native brook trout beneath these falls, grateful for the oxygen bath during hot months.

Perhaps the most striking feature of Pounding Mill Creek is its testimony to a concentrated effort to save streams as small as this one. High up the mountain where it becomes a shallow summertime trickle, there are still trout-stocking signs posted, along with one poster reading, "Save Den Trees." FR 125 rides along the crest of Fore Mountain, in some places looking down a cliff to the tips of hundred-foot chestnut oaks. Little traveled, except by a few timber trucks, this one-lane drive is a treat in itself, leading eventually to other fly-fishing opportunities along Smith Creek near Clifton Forge.

Directions: From I-64 westbound take the US 220 cutoff, proceeding into the Covington city limits. Turn right on East Dolly Ann Drive, which is VA(s) 625, paved at first but rapidly becoming dirt and gravel where state maintenance ends. It then becomes FR 125 paralleling Pounding Mill Creek to the top of Fore Mountain.

SMITH CREEK (ALLEGHENY COUNTY)

STREAM TYPE: Freestone • USGS Clifton Forge • DeLORME 52

Unlike most small mountain streams, Smith Creek has enough flow to allow fishing even during the low-water months. The upper section contains a series of natural stone sluiceways entrapping pools of water four or five feet deep. Because of the glassy clarity of these sluices, fish can spot even the slightest careless move, but a camouflaged, cautious stalk from downstream can bring you within casting distance. Terrestrials are the main food supply here, as the creek has few mayfly hatches on its swift surface.

What impresses you most about Smith Creek is the multitude of brook trout shapes darting upstream in nearly every pool. These are both natives and holdovers, with brook trout only being stocked here. The upper section flows through deep woods, where the aroma of aging damp leaves overcomes the occasional unpleasant wafting from Covington's paper mill, some miles to the southwest. Although closely paralleled by VA 606, this colorful stream shows little sign of fishing pressure. It displays one classic small waterfall and plunge pool after another. This frequency of irresistible fishing spots may explain the good holdover and native population, dispersing pressure throughout the entire length of the Smith. Another asset of this stream is the regulated stretch downstream, which may be the best fishing of all— certainly when it comes to brown trout.

Despite the time of day, the weather, or pressure of scheduling, there is no choice but to fish these bubbling emerald pools. There is simply no alternative. It is surprising to find small, voracious brookies in each pool in sufficient quantity to keep one fishing for over an hour without rehooking one. With the enthusiasm and appetite of the young of any species, these vibrant little trout clear the water after a Letort Hopper when it's lifted from the surface. What's even more encouraging is to see the larger brethren of these small members of the congregation at the last moment turn away from the temptation of a wet-fly hackle. Such action can be had at midday even during the heat of August, when the coolness on one's bare shins provides refreshing relief.

These are all lively, healthy fish, with plenty of dace, small crayfish, gray spiders, and moths providing nourishment. There is an abundance of these and other insects in the crevices of the purple shale lining the banks. One caution, however, concerns the tendency of the thin stone to present a seemingly sturdy foothold only to crumble like cake frosting when stepped on. Without careful choice of steps, this could lead to a tumble down the steep bank into a sudden, breath-robbing bath—fine in August, perhaps, but a little too startling in April.

Directions: From I-81 take the US 220 exit north to Clifton Forge. Go through town to VA(s) 606 which proceeds north of Clifton Forge to Smith Creek, which is regulated from the town to the water-treatment plant. Above the reservoir is a walk-in stretch.

SPRING RUN

STREAM TYPE: Limestone • USGS Williamsville • DeLORME 65

The outstanding feature of Spring Run is that it is the outflow of the state trout hatchery at Coursey Springs. The stream is not a part of the hatchery but is stocked regularly from it. One might be tempted to think fishing Spring Run is like dropping a fly into one of the hatchery holding ponds. Nothing could be further from the truth.

These are wary fish, looking up at you from the diamond-clear water, ready to scamper into the aquatic weeds at the slightest movement. It is recommended that one stalk these rainbows just as you would wild trout. And if you see the faint outlines of fish finning calmly in the current, chances are they have seen you first and have not the slightest inclination to take your fly. A much more productive strategy is to cast upstream next to beds of cress which with luck will screen you from sight.

From the hatchery dam downstream to where Spring Run empties into the Cowpasture River is around 900 yards. It is no hardship to walk a careful distance away from the stream down to the confluence and then fish back upstream. Where the creek empties into the Cowpasture there is some deep water, and sizable trout may be hiding away from the fishing traffic. But don't be surprised at hooking into a two-foot fallfish, which may give you a "brown trout" fight for a brief period before tiring.

This is purely a meadow stream, flowing quietly down a slight gradient, with long stretches of quiet but relatively shallow water between. Terrestrials are sometimes the preferred lures, particularly when hoppers are observed in the streamside fields. Spring Run rainbows sometimes strike at your leader knot, which some theorize indicates a preference for gnats. Smaller flies do appear to be more successful than large, and casting is simplified by lack of bushes to hang up backcasts.

A bonus of stalking Spring Run trout is the opportunity to observe their hatchery brethren and see what they are siphoning off the surface of Coursey Spring. Occasionally an osprey will remove a link from the food chain, carrying off a small rainbow from a holding pond for its breakfast. The hatchery opens at 8:00 A.M., along with fishing privileges at Spring Run. Fishing stops at 3:00 P.M., and the hatchery road is chained shut to visitors at 3:30.

Directions: Spring Run may be reached via VA(s) 678, which turns east off of VA 39 just north of Millboro Springs. Follow 678 14½ miles almost to Williamsville and turn right at the Coursey Springs Fish Cultural Station sign. For those planning to fish Bath and Highland counties, Spring Run is a good starting point for determining which mayfly hatches are on the streams or which terrestrials are being taken.

4

James River Drainage

As you turn east off of Interstate 81 onto I-64 toward Charlottesville, the terrain is gentle and rolling, with mostly farmland in sight. The highway begins a sudden climb up Afton Mountain, and at Rockfish Gap you are suddenly on top of the Blue Ridge, where the Skyline Drive and Blue Ridge Parkway join. For the trout angler this is decision time. You can elect to turn north and explore some of the thirty native trout streams within the Shenandoah National Park boundaries, or you can turn south and follow the Blue Ridge Parkway toward the Montebello Fish Cultural Station and the St. Mary's Wilderness Area with its river of the same name.

At Irish Gap on the parkway, you can turn east and discover the upper Piney River, especially welcome on a warm day, when you can fish beneath the cooling caverns of hemlock. The Pedlar River watershed, leading down to the Lynchburg Reservoir, offers not only the Pedlar, but also Irish Creek and enough other small streams to fill a day.

The streams in this area are relatively sedate, leading down to pastureland and small villages, unlike the area west of I-81 where the mountains dominate. In fact, some of the top fly-fishing in the James River drainage is found in the suburbs of Waynesboro, where a regulated stretch of the South River meanders between clipped suburban lawns. Also falling within the James River drainage are the

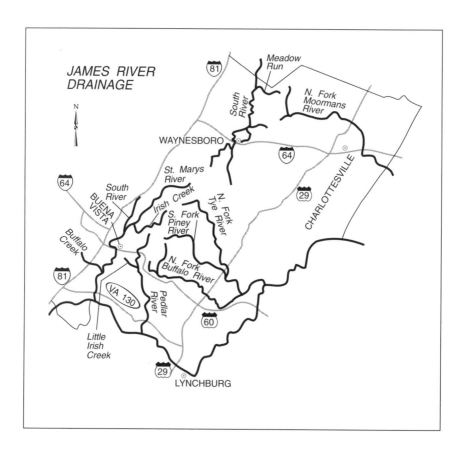

southernmost streams of Shenandoah National Park. Two of the best, Meadow Run and the North Fork of the Moorman's River, are within easy reach of both Waynesboro and Charlottesville.

BUFFALO RIVER (AMHERST COUNTY)

STREAM TYPE: Freestone • USGS Forks of Buffalo • DeLorme 54

The Buffalo River's North Fork is sometimes more accurately labeled Buffalo Creek, being one of the Blue Ridge watershed's typical moderate- to high-gradient smaller streams. It is not to be confused with the special-regulation stretch of another Buffalo Creek, in Rockbridge County.

Be prepared to make a day of it on the Buffalo, beginning with some slow grinding of your four-wheel-drive gears up the random boulder roadbed at the end of VA(s) 635. At some point your spinal column and truck springs reach a point of no return. But the wear and tear on tires is more than compensated by the ravenous wild trout population of this stream, many of them in the eight- to ten-inch category.

> AUTHOR'S NOTE: My first experience with the Buffalo was in mid-March, a couple of weeks after the season's opening. There was not another soul around, and very little debris from opening day activities. Forty-five minutes of casting a series of wet minnow imitations produced only one small brookie and a twisted left ankle. Sitting beside a plunge pool, nursing sprained ligaments, I noticed a March Brown hovering over the water. Tying on a fly of the same name, I cast from a seated position, immediately hooking a seven-inch trout. That small pool yielded four more brookies, none of them going the required nine inches, but all surprisingly strong for their size.
>
> Moving downstream, where I had previously been skunked, I picked up some eight- to ten-inch fish where small tributaries fed in. As usual these more mature trout were warier, and in many cases looked my March Brown over carefully only to give it a tail slap. This one fly landed over two dozen fish before it was frazzled beyond deception.

This is not a wading stream; rather, be prepared for some rockclimbing along the banks. Many of the boulders along the way are over ten feet in height, and these towering slabs shape the character of the Buffalo, forming the most perfect plunge pools in this area of the Blue Ridge. Within almost every pool is a lively population of brook trout, constantly on the move because of the short supply of minnows. In some cases giant rocks rest at the water's edge, bordered by narrow strips of sand and gravel. One way to use these is to cast around the corner of a boulder onto unseen stretches of clear water. This gets tricky, as the only indication of a dry-fly strike is the slight upstream tightening of line or sound of a splash.

Another technique is to climb atop a stone slab and edge your way carefully—very carefully—over a pool. From this high perch you can cast upstream onto clear and relatively shallow water without being

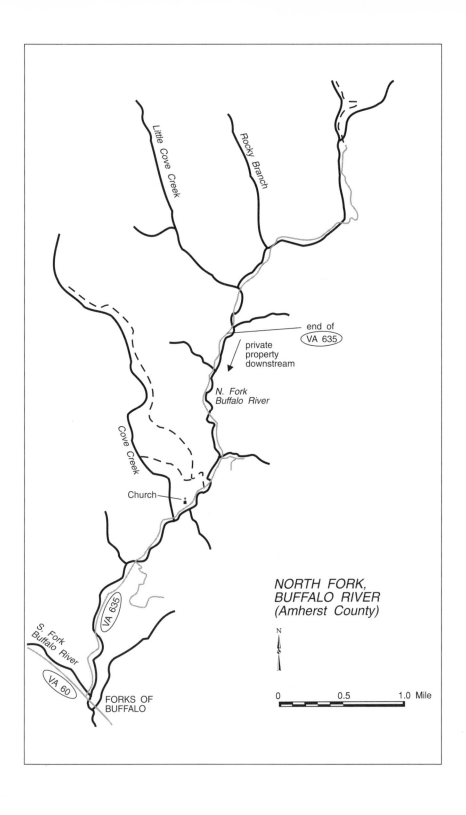

Little Cove Creek

Rocky Branch

end of
VA 635

private
property
downstream

N. Fork
Buffalo River

Cove Creek

Church

NORTH FORK,
BUFFALO RIVER
(Amherst County)

N

VA 635

S. Fork
Buffalo River

VA 60

FORKS OF
BUFFALO

0   0.5   1.0 Mile

spotted. The terrain and gradient of the Buffalo is reminiscent of a number of the Shenandoah National Park's wild trout streams. Only here in this remote corner of the George Washington National Forest there is a better chance of finding yourself all alone on the stream.

Special Regulations: On the North Fork of the Buffalo and its tributaries within the George Washington National Forest, fishing is restricted to single-hook artificial lures; creel limit 6 fish per day; all fish less than 9 inches long must immediately be returned unharmed to the water; possession of fish less than 9 inches long is illegal; possession of bait on this water is illegal. All portions of the Buffalo described here are within the George Washington National Forest.

Directions: From I-81, take VA 60 east through Buena Vista to Forks of Buffalo, where VA(s) 635 turns north. Follow 635 to the end, at which the road becomes little more than a trail into the George Washington National Forest.

IRISH CREEK

STREAM TYPE: Freestone • USGS Cornwall, Montebello
DeLorme 54

There are frequent gravel turnoffs above the stream as VA(s) 603 climbs South Mountain, most of them overlooking stunning visual treats, with white pines marching to the stream, whose banks are heavily bordered with wildflowers. At first glance, the Irish, not to be confused with the Little Irish, appears to be the ideal of every mountain-stream connoisseur. And for the most part it is. But there are some ugly contrasts, such as a rusty old refrigerator with its feet sticking out of what otherwise would be some eminently fishable tailwater. This is an infrequent sight, and throughout the George Washington National Forest property the rangers patrol conscientiously. But there are some stretches of private land, and as sad testimony to the human condition, old tires and assorted other rubbish have been pushed over the bank into heartbreakingly beautiful trout water there. The desecration is brief, so pass through this put-and-take area up to where South Mountain's real treasures lie.

The water is crystalline, so trout may be spotted easily, even to the point that one can see what they are feeding on—quick, swirling movements after minnows, tail-up searching after nymphs along the bottom. Mayflies predominate, mostly March Browns and Hendricksons. The problem is finding a pool quiet enough to reveal the surface feeders.

Mother Nature has provided frequent rockslides, forming sluices through which the Irish rushes at a decent depth. At convenient points the National Forest Authority has constructed walls from the abundant riverjacks (smooth stones) enclosed in wire mesh, protecting the stream's banks. As the road becomes steep, there are three levels of rock walls forming a backdrop for the Irish's thumbnail Niagara. Here is a treat for the eye, plus a twenty-foot-deep basin of swirling water below containing trout large enough to break a four-pound leader without showing themselves. This is fruitful territory for a larger nymph or streamer, such as a Hair Wing or Wooly Bugger.

Because of the water's clarity, a fisherman may be sure that the downstream fish have spotted him just after his head pops up over a stone wall. Fishing upstream helps, as does visiting the Irish after a spring rain has turned it milky.

Overlooking the Irish during a lunch break, you'd think it impossible that anyone should ever tire of these emerald and crystal mountain gems. Their fragility is also apparent, however, as is the need for gentle treatment of the trout and their habitat. Fly-fishing here is an exercise in intricacy, with little opportunity to lash out with thirty-foot casts as on the big waters, such as Virginia's Jackson River.

Far upstream the Irish begins to lose its boisterous identity and comes to look like any number of other small Appalachian mountain gems, if you discount the occasional mallard drake floating about irritably. In early spring there probably would be a hen on the nest somewhere nearby. Here you will find wild trout.

Two notes of caution: copperheads have been spotted among the fissures of the endless boulder piles that contain the Irish. So take your eye off the fly occasionally when taking a step. Secondly, the gravelly foothold on rock shelves fifty feet above the stream requires some concentration. As with many smaller trout waters, wading seldom if ever becomes necessary on the Irish. If one chooses to enter the water, rock ledges are usually covered with gritty sand or gravel, making for easy footing.

Shell and claw leavings from a raccoon's supper may indicate tying on a crayfish imitation. High up on the Irish's headwaters, however, the smaller native fish will have trouble swallowing a larger lure, so you may get strikes without hooking the fish. The abundance of crayfish may explain why your perfectly presented black gnat is being ignored by the trout. High on the Irish you are in hemlock country, and the dimly filtered light even at midday encourages moths to fly over the stream, making your white moth fair game.

Driving up VA(s) 603, one begins to wonder if the abundance of tempting fishing waters will ever end, with the mountain spring branches continually falling down into the creek. Where they empty in, there is a proliferation of underwater life forms, not only crayfish but also mayfly and stonefly nymphs and small black snails. A dry-fly fisherman may be temporarily thwarted on the Irish. But there's no reason he can't switch to a Pheasant Wing Nymph or green beetle.

The luck of the Irish is that it has one picture-perfect little trout glen after the other. The higher up South Mountain one goes, the better chance of encountering wily little native brook trout.

Directions: Take I-81 to Exit 53. Turn north onto US 11 past the Maple Hall Country Inn and go to the Sam Houston Wayside where a sign indicates VA(s) 785 leading to VA(s) 716. Take 716, go left on 706, right on 710, and come out at the Concord Church of the Brethren. Turn right on VA(s) 608 paralleling the South River downstream to where it joins Irish Creek. Turn left here on VA(s) 603 and drive up South Mountain, fishing as many alluring holes and rapids as you can fit into the day.

LITTLE IRISH CREEK

STREAM TYPE: Freestone • USGS Buena Vista • DeLorme 54

Among a maze of dirt and gravel roads east of the Pedlar River is a stream which is a delight to the eyes. The Little Irish stair-steps down to the Pedlar in a series of cameo cascades. Each of these waterfalls has worn a hole in the granite ten or fifteen feet deep, and within these are trout to be had. The idea is to approach cautiously and let the natural downward current carry your nymph to the bottom. Brooks of

The author, just before spontaneously releasing a nice rainbow back into its freestone pool.

surprising size can be caught in these waterfall lees. Between casts in the spring you can admire the pink trillium growing on the banks.

As you follow the Little Irish upstream, the stair-steps become less dramatic, and instead of waterfalls become short stretches of riffles ending in five-foot-deep potholes. Each of these is a different challenge, to be studied from a distance and then approached taking maximum advantage of cover. This is not big water by any means. But a shiny-bodied Number 20 black ant eased over partly submerged logs can make your day on the Little Irish.

Directions: Little Irish Creek is an interesting contrast to the Pedlar River, and both streams are close enough together to be easily fished in a day. About six miles east of Buena Vista on US 60, turn south on FR 39. Follow FR 39 down the Pedlar nearly to the southern end of the Lynchburg Reservoir and turn west on FR 311. This one-lane gravel road parallels the Little Irish for several miles, and likely holes may be scouted from the road with ease.

MEADOW RUN

STREAM TYPE: Freestone • USGS Crimora • DeLorme 67

This small park stream runs very low during the summer, yet maintains a surprising population of brook trout. Despite a scarcity of hatches there is a moderate amount of surface feeding on a variety of terrestrials. And there is a heavy concentration of blacknose dace.

For those who prefer solitude with their fishing, Meadow Run has plenty. Access to the stream requires over three miles of hiking, most of it on a smooth but steep trail well maintained by the Shenandoah National Park service. Allow enough time to climb the Shenandoah Range back out before dark, and wear strong hiking shoes or boots. Also, be at somewhat better than "couch potato" fitness. Waders are not a must but will be a slight convenience when the stream is running at capacity.

No hunting is permitted, so game proliferates along the trail. It is impossible not to run across small animals, turkey, deer, and an occasional bear. There are signs posted in the park warning "This Is

Bear Country," so don't be surprised to run across a bruin while you're fishing. These are park bears, accustomed to hikers, but possessing the same muscle, teeth, and claws as wild bears anywhere. So some judgment is required when encountering that rare bear which does not immediately flee from a human, usually a mother with cubs.

> AUTHOR'S NOTE: In mid-September of 1990, I was fishing the upstream section of Meadow Run when a slight rustle caused me to look up. Twenty-five yards downstream was a 200-pound female black bear and her two cubs. Scenting me, she stopped and took a hard look in my direction, while the cubs peeked around her knickers. Then she started toward me in a determined fashion. Armed only with a walking stick and a seven-foot Shakespeare Wonderod, I selected one of the few uninviting options open to me. Crouching toward her, I struck the stones in the trail with my staff and shouted at the top of my lungs. This frightened the cubs, who laid back their ears and ran. She turned toward them, then back toward me, and after a moment of consideration decided to follow the cubs. The thunder of her feet striking the ground is a sound I will never forget, and I will forever be grateful that the sound was fading rather than approaching.

As with any jump-across mountain stream, the following rules apply on Meadow Run: go slow; stay low; blend in (camouflage clothing works best, but at the very least wear "earth colors" which blend in with the background); stay thin (referring to leaders, of course: despite the tendency of 6X to kink and become invisible, the results are worth the aggravation).

Along the lower stretch of Meadow Run to the Shenandoah National Park boundary, the brooks are smaller. Nudging the submerged roots of a downed tree can produce a family of eighteen or twenty trout ranging from nine inches down to "pinkie" fingerling size. They appear instantly, and hang immobile like so many aquarium fish, gazing curiously at fishermen who at that point can kiss goodbye to any chance of catching them.

Paradoxically, farther upstream the fish are larger, although not as numerous. This may be due to the steeper gradient up the mountainside, which produces deeper holes beneath the cascades. Hatches are practically nonexistent, although they're more likely to occur down on the valley floor than up in bear country. Small terrestrials, even Number 22 jassids, are preferred. Meadow Run brook trout are terrestrial feeders, and lures should approximate ants, beetles, spiders, and small moths.

Directions: From within the Shenandoah National Park, drive to Skyline Drive milepost 92 and park there in the Wildcat Ridge parking area. Then follow the Wildcat Ridge Trail down 2.7 miles where it intersects with the Riprap Trail. The Riprap Trail follows Meadow Run downstream to the left and upstream if you turn right.

Below the park boundary Meadow Run's banks are private and heavily posted, and access from below can be gained only by asking individual landowners. It hardly matters, because these Shenandoah streams are at their best within the park boundaries, where their hike-in access from the Skyline Drive preserves their solitude and fishing quality.

MOORMAN'S RIVER, NORTH FORK

STREAM TYPE: Freestone • USGS Brown's Cove • DeLorme 67

One is struck by the imposing concrete dam across the lower Moorman's River, high enough to contain the water supply for the city of Charlottesville. Here there is no hunting, trapping, swimming, or camping, and fires are prohibited. But there is fishing, and the few people you meet are probably trout-fishing purists. The restrictions have led to an abundance of game, and it should be no surprise to see a fawn in early September, wearing summer red and spots, easing down the road toward you. Without fear of people, the deer approach close enough to imitate dogs getting ready to sniff your trouser leg.

The small feeder roads like VA(s) 614, around the periphery of the Shenandoah National Park, afford perhaps the best look at the trout potential. Shenandoah is said to have the heaviest traffic of our national parks, perhaps because of its proximity to eastern population centers. Even during the height of the vacation season, however, one may approach the Moorman's from the lower boundary through the

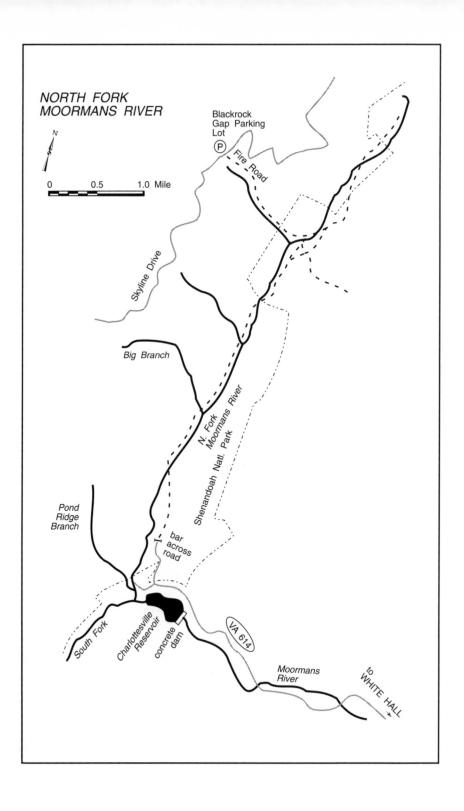

NORTH FORK
MOORMANS RIVER

N

0   0.5   1.0 Mile

Blackrock
Gap Parking
Lot
P

Fire Road

Skyline Drive

Big Branch

N. Fork Moormans River

Shenandoah Natl. Park

Pond
Ridge
Branch

bar
across
road

Charlottesville Reservoir

concrete dam

South Fork

VA 614

Moormans
River

to WHITE HALL

seldom seen countryside in comparative solitude. Along the streams there may be a few fishermen, but mainly you see Appalachian Trail hikers and other environmentally sensitive visitors.

At the tail of the reservoir you will see the first state trout-stocking signs. Above the dam, the North Fork of the Moorman's becomes a typical Shenandoah drainage stream, very low and clear during the hot months. Fishing is possible but demanding at low water, and early spring is the right time to experience the Moorman's. Even when the water is low, however, this stream is cold enough to support a lively trout population, including some nice browns.

The road upstream becomes a series of ditches with thin plateaus between, making a four-wheeler desirable. After a couple of miles there is a bar blocking vehicle travel, with a sign indicating that all-terrain vehicles and trail bikes are prohibited. The message reads further that the Moorman's is a catch-and-release stream from this point on. As might be expected, more and larger trout are spotted in the catch-and-release section. The sight of a trout finning in the pool fifty feet below you normally means that you might as well forget it; he has seen you as well. It is advisable to retreat slowly and approach the pool again from behind cover, even if that means casting blind over a boulder. These are wary fish, particularly during low water.

Turning over stones usually fails to produce any nymphs or stonefly larvae in the downstream section, but there is an abundance of shiners, crayfish, snails, and terrestrial insects. Farther upstream there is some surface feeding, and the food, cover, and pool depths are generally better near the top. An ideal way to see the Moorman's is to park two vehicles, one above the dam and the other at Blackrock Gap, then fish upstream to the Skyline Drive.

Special Regulations: From the Shenandoah National Park boundary, this is catch-and-release water: fishing restricted to artificial flies with single, barbless hooks; all fish must be handled carefully and returned immediately to the water; possession of fish, at any time, is illegal.

Directions: From I-64 east toward Charlottesville, take the exit at US 250 and follow it east to Yancey Mills and Sassy Lotus. From there take VA 240 to VA(s) 810 north. Follow 810 to the intersection with VA(s) 614 at White Hall. Turn left on 614, also known as Sugar Hollow

Road. From a fairly good two-lane pavement, 614 becomes a 15-mph dirt road leading to the Charlottesville Reservoir, formed by damming Moorman's River.

To reach the stream from above, inside the Shenandoah National Park, go to the Blackrock Gap parking area at milepost 87 of the Skyline Drive. Cross the highway and walk down the North Fork Moorman's River Road. Eventually you'll pass through some private grazing land where hiking and fishing are permitted.

PEDLAR RIVER

STREAM TYPE: Freestone • USGS Buena Vista • DeLorme 54

Fishing the Pedlar takes one through an exhibit of the variety of trout angling in Virginia. As you move upstream, totally different habitats are successively revealed, reminding one of other spots on other streams. The bottom is gravel and small stones, providing good footing throughout the streambed.

There are constant reminders that a large beaver colony is lurking somewhere in the woods nearby. Sizable trees are felled, leaving the characteristic pointed stumps cut by beaver incisors. An occasional twig dam spans the Pedlar, behind which the stream has silted up, making for less than ideal trout habitat—unlike the effect of beaver dams on other streams.

At the George Washington National Forest Wayside, the Pedlar is barely wide enough to deserve the label River. But this stretch contains some deep holes, and from the many boot tracks appears to be heavily fished early in the season when brook and rainbow are stocked. Fishing upstream to a steel bridge, one observes a sharp change in the Pedlar's character. The stream narrows, holes are shallower, there is an abundance of rapids, and the streamside paths are less worn.

At the Oronoco equipment shelter, upstream within sight of the bridge, there is a dirt lane which dead-ends quickly. From there it is a short walk to a Pedlar somewhat different from the wider area downstream. It reverts to a mountain-spring creek here, calling for an assortment of small nymphs and wet flies. There is an abundance of small minnows in the backwaters, and minnow imitations such as a small sinking Muddler can be effective.

Following FR 39 downstream takes you to some steep and relatively remote terrain where there is a good holdover brown population. Fingerling browns are stocked in the upstream section, which remains mostly put-and-take.

Directions: Take US 60 for about six miles east from Buena Vista, then turn north on VA(s) 605. At National Forest stop sign Number 76, turn left to a rest area on the stream bank. Continuing farther on VA(s) 605 brings you to private land where stream access is prohibited. You can also take FR 39, a gravel road which follows the Pedlar downstream to the Lynchburg Reservoir.

PINEY RIVER, SOUTH FORK

Stream type: Freestone • USGS Massies Mill • DeLorme 54

Driving in from the lower reaches of the Piney River may tend to be a discouraging experience. The stream is jealously posted, with no fishing being the dominant theme, although someone is obviously doing a thorough job of private trout management with weirs and channel deflectors. Farther upstream on VA(s) 827 the water emerges from the George Washington National Forest, and there is public access plus stocking.

There are long, quiet stretches of Piney River just inside the National Forest where surface feeding may be observed. For the most part, though, this stretch is a rocky spillway through the mountains, with stair-step cascades and pools. Still, this is a put-and-take stretch.

For solitude of the most sublime nature, the country around the upper headwaters of this stream is the place to be, particularly during the hot months. A mature forest bends over the cascades, completing the coolness. For some reason this section of the Piney River shows little sign of wear. There is not a speck of trash, and the paths do not show any recent wading-boot tracks. Is it just possible that this is one of those streams which come near deserving the label "untouched"?

True, there is no truly untouched public trout stream in the eastern United States, but in this part of Virginia the Piney comes close. It is heartening to find a trout fishery of this quality so close to population and so relatively untainted by the detritus of civilization.

In some cases the whopping size of trout which make a pass at your Hare's Ear nymph can be startling. These are veterans of many seasons, so they don't always fall for even the best Coachman or nymph.

Unless you have plenty of time, don't bother to trek into the upper Piney. At every turn in the road there is another irresistible pool below which cries out to be fished. Typically there are great panlike expanses of granite which have deep basins carved into them by the millennia of cascading water. Below the boulders, in the foaming green turbulence, are some of the most gorgeously colored native brook trout anywhere in this state. Occasional pods of smaller natives show no reluctance in taking whatever is offered, although a wet Olive Dun may prove most consistent.

Showing up as jet black shapes beneath the surface, when taken from the water these eight-inch gems literally glow with purple-red spots and gold flecks equaled only by high-grade ore, the colors of nature found only in spring-water native brookies. Even the most hardened game hog would have difficulty killing one of these specimens.

Directions: Turn off the Blue Ridge Parkway near Buena Vista onto US 60 and follow it east for approximately 2.5 miles. At Oronoco take a left on VA(s) 634 and go to Alto, continuing on VA(s) 634 until it becomes FR 63 at the point where public access begins within the George Washington National Forest. FR 63 parallels the South Fork of the Piney for a considerable distance.

SOUTH RIVER

STREAM TYPE: Freestone • USGS Cornwall • DeLorme 54

VA(s) 710 leads you past the Concord Church of the Brethren, to VA(s) 608. The paved road alongside South River makes this stream almost feasible to cast over from the bed of a pickup truck. It is accessible, and fishing pressure is heavy. This far upstream it doesn't really deserve to be called a river, and is more an overgrown spring creek. It's hardly even fifty feet across. Some concrete low-water bridges, mostly washed away, provide good trout cover, though, so it's a worthwhile stream. One suggestion: because of its manicured banks and easy accessibility from a busy road, you may improve your chances by making a wide circle downstream and fishing the tailwater upstream.

Around the village of Midvale, the gradient is steeper and the pools are deeper. Downstream is stocked heavily, and it might be assumed that the bait fishermen have been here. But wait—below a bridge is a tempting bit of tailwater which has been scanned by truckloads of fishermen. One can imagine the same conversation being repeated over and over: "Naw. Don't stop here. Everybody fishes at the bridge. It's bound to be fished out. Let's go down to where Irish Creek empties in." And yet this highly visible pool contains at least one tackle-busting brookie which attacks a weighted Number 18 Muddler Minnow as if it were a sworn enemy. But that's what makes the South River worth trying: the frequency of rapids with good green holes beneath them, passed up by fishermen headed for the more rugged Irish Creek up the mountainside. Where the two streams meet in the flatlands, there is a sufficient flow of water to deserve the name River, perhaps not in Idaho, but certainly in western Virginia.

Just south of Waynesboro the South runs through a residential area, where it maintains its identity as a trout fishery. There is a fishable-size stocking here, with a delayed harvest. The stream is open for fishing October 1 and closes May 15. Some consider this unlikely area to be one of the best fly-fishing spots in the state.

Directions: Take Exit 53 from I-81, just north of Lexington. Follow US 11 north to the Sam Houston Wayside, turn right on VA(s) 785, which

Tammy Hiner, wife of entomologist and part-time trout guide Steve Hiner, demonstrates her fly-fishing skill.

leads to 716. Go left on VA(s) 706 to 710, which leads past the Concord Church to the first public access. Turn right on 608 and follow the river downstream.

ST. MARY'S RIVER

STREAM TYPE: Freestone (acidified) • USGS Big Levels
DeLorme 54

Perhaps the greatest plus for St. Mary's River is the surroundings, a national wilderness area where the natural environment is energetically preserved—the St. Mary's Wilderness Area of the George Washington National Forest. Once you walk through the weathered turnstile, you're into a Virginia which might have existed a century ago. Civilization is left behind, with strict provisos that no vehicles are allowed, including trailbikes. It's a no-impact area, from which all trash must be transported out.

The St. Mary's is a pleasant enough little stream—a brook, a branch, a creek, but by no stretch of the imagination a full-grown river. Even when the spring freshets swell this stream to bursting, it's still small water. At the entrance to the wilderness area it's difficult to spot the small native trout which call this stream their home. Here it is accessible to all who step from their vehicles and begin casting.

Farther upstream—quite a hike upstream, past Sugar Tree Branch to where Mine Branch Creek empties in, and up to Hogback Creek— the true nature of this little stream makes itself known. It's a place for dapping a fly for native brookies, in small potholes and at the foot of rapids which gurgle rather than roar. Small black ants, gnats, or perhaps an Adams Number 12 are called for.

Get to the St. Mary's in time to hike a mile or two before making your first cast. And once you're in the wilderness area, it's not a bad idea to have a lunch and something to drink in your creel. There are rockslides, miniature canyons, cliffs, rock formations, and a side trail to St. Mary's Falls, all of which may occupy time otherwise spent fishing. For those who wish to fish all the way through, the trail ends with an intersection of FR 478, where a second vehicle can be left.

Special Regulations: On this water and its tributaries, fishing is restricted to single-hook artificial lures; all fish less than 9 inches long must be handled carefully and immediately returned unharmed to the water; possession of fish less than 9 inches long on this water is illegal.

Directions: Take Exit 54 from I-81 and go east to US 11. At Steele's Tavern take VA 56 east. Just before reaching the town of Vesuvius, turn left on VA(s) 608. Then turn right off of 608 onto FR 41 and follow it to the parking area, which is a dead end. Just to your right will be the St. Mary's River, and ahead is the entrance to the St. Mary's National Wilderness Area.

TYE RIVER, NORTH FORK

STREAM TYPE: Freestone • USGS Big Levels • DeLorme 54

Upstream this relatively small water is posted with unmistakable No Fishing signs. Four miles downstream from the intersection with VA(s) 687 state stocking signs indicate it is open to public fishing. There are some deep holes, with numerous small streams tumbling into the Tye from the mountains on either side. The water gives new meaning to the word "pure," and is crystal clear even in midsummer, maintaining a fairly good flow during the hot, dry months. In shaded pools, particularly where feeder streams empty in, there is a good chance of running into native brook trout.

Along VA(s) 687 there are numerous slick-worn paths leading to the greener, deeper holes, and there's no doubt they have been fished heavily. Perhaps the saving feature of the Tye is its tendency to drop suddenly into a series of gorges hundreds of feet beneath the roadbed. The stream becomes next to inaccessible. Only someone with the time to fish into these ravines, or the daring to hand-over-hand down into them, will benefit from the rainbows which hold over from season to season. The brook trout there are natives.

The stream is filled with a mixed bag of minnows, which fight over your smaller flies for the privilege of hooking themselves. An over-turned rock yields several types of nymphs, of surprising size, and for some reason there is an absence of stonefly larva. A Hare's Ear nymph comes closest to replicating the live forms found here.

About five miles downstream you run through a row of summer cabins barricaded with posted signs. This may pose a problem, because most of this property is absentee-owned, and thus it can be impossible to request permission to fish. VA(s) 687 eventually merges with US 56, and following the road east takes you alongside a segment of the Tye which is thirty to forty feet across. The stream is stocked alongside the pavement but flows rather slowly and would appear to be a little warm for trout after mid-June.

Directions: Between Lexington and Staunton southbound, take Exit 54 off I-81 and turn left on US 11. Travel to Steele's Tavern and turn right there on VA 56. Follow 56 east through Vesuvius and turn left on VA(s) 686. Turn off to the right onto VA(s) 687, which parallels the North Fork of the Tye River downstream.

5

Roanoke Valley

The city of Roanoke's claim to be Trout Capital of Virginia is based upon geography rather than the proximity of premier streams. There are fishable streams nearby, one being the Roanoke River, which has been cleaned up sufficiently to produce downtown rainbow trout. And within an hour's drive of the city limits there is considerable stocked stream mileage on waters such as Jennings, Potts, Barbour's and the privately managed Cascades Creeks, plus some lesser know wild trout fisheries. Most of these suffer from their proximity to dense population, and on an opening day Jennings Creek sees a dozen fishermen perched upon boulders around their common favorite hole, glowering at one another. But drive for two or three hours, and you're on the banks of streams with few or no boot-trampled areas.

The 500-mile eastern flank of the southern Appalachians, better known as the Blue Ridge, drapes down from Pennsylvania Amish country all the way into northern Georgia. If it were a diamond necklace, its central pendant would be the Roanoke Valley. The Blue Ridge Parkway grazes the edge of the Roanoke city limits, and from it small gorges and ravines may be reached. Flowing through them are laurel-shaded waterways on which mayflies hatch seven months of the year.

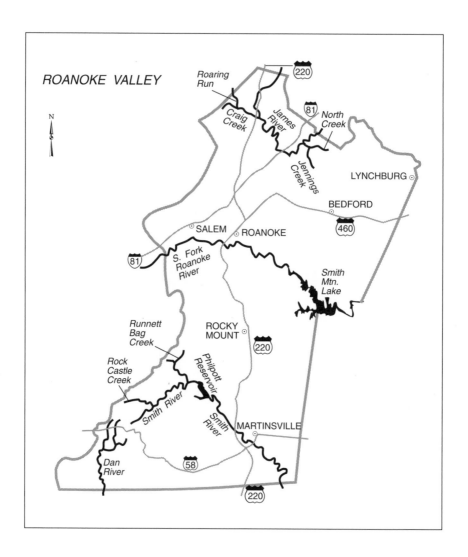

Some but not all of these waters are covered in the section below. If you're looking for wild trout fly-fishing at its purest, one good way to find it is to trace the popular stocked streams up toward their sources. Here the angling traffic thins out, the litter line ends, and for those with a taste for small mountain brook fishing, these freestone headwaters offer some challenging miniature plunge pools and rapids.

DAN RIVER

STREAM TYPE: Freestone • USGS Meadows of Dan • DeLorme 25

The Dan is one of those unobtrusive streams one passes when driving through the area called Southside Virginia. For the most part it is a sluggish, silted, ditchlike stream flowing past occasional dilapidated clay-chinked log tobacco barns, and not worth a second look. But turn upstream on VA(s) 648, and behold a slow miracle taking place. As you proceed toward the Pinnacles of Dan, the blowsy Dan River slowly upgrades its character to a clear, virginal stream more and more bespeaking trout.

This is a pattern repeated time after time with Appalachian trout fisheries. In the "flatlands" they mingle their original mountain source water with ingredients that would cause a carp to scarf—fertilizer, pesticides, cattle droppings, and you name it. But the rewards of following even the most diseased rivers toward their sources can be dramatic. Often they become tumbling, blue-green and white fisheries which can hold you for a full day. Such a stream is the Dan.

As 648 begins its climb into the foothills, rapids and swift pools appear. There is a vestige of silt, but it disappears as you go farther up the mountain, following the stream through wooded areas. Because of its ready accessibility from the roadside, the Dan remains a put-and-take stream lower down the mountainside. It's a comparatively large freestone river, averaging seventy-five to 100 feet across. At the base of the Pinnacles of Dan, there is a hydroelectric plant, and here the character of the Dan River changes dramatically.

Looking two miles up the Alpine face of the Pinnacles, you can make out a thin black crescent, mottled with green. This is a power-generating dam, clinging to the mountainside, sending a flume underground to the generating plant. Behind the two-story brick hydroelectric facility down below lies that half of the Dan River not captured by the underground flume, following the original streambed. In this unlikely setting is one of the more spectacular trout waters in southwest Virginia, with classic falls and deeps, containing green water occasionally disappearing into the black holes tunneled out by centuries of fast water.

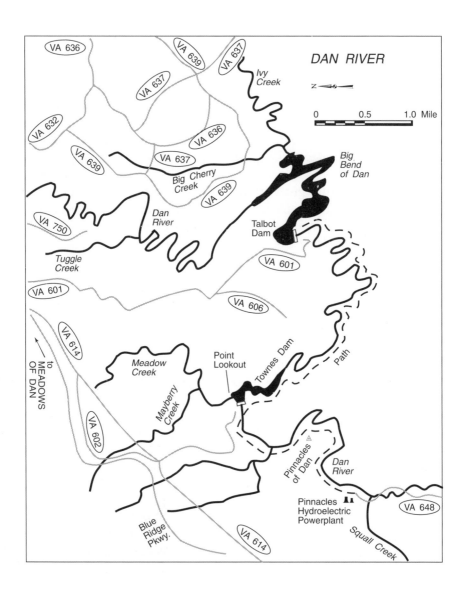

Author's Note: On my first trip to the upper Dan River, I stopped at the generating plant to obtain written permission for fishing and to ask the length of the path leading upstream from the road's end. A lanky, bearded Patrick Countyan looked my sexagenarian physique up and down and replied, "As fur upstream as you wanta go." This turned out to be a total of two miles up the side of the Pinnacles.

At the first Stolich-clear pool, I paused to observe four sizable brown trout sizing me up. At first they whipped around in the short, alert circle which usually lets me know I have been spotted and there's no way they'll take any lure. Since they soon returned and held in a steady pod, however, I tossed in a Muddler Minnow, which sent one of the four scurrying for a rock hideout. I tried another cast, dropping the Muddler just under their noses, and one of them grabbed it, much to my surprise and that of his two companions, who streaked off in a hurry. The fish turned out to be a chunky brown, much heavier than its fourteen inches would have indicated. Beautifully marked, it was bright gold all the way under its belly, with black circles defining magenta centers. A brown trout maven later asked me if it were a German or Loch Leven, and I answered that I honestly didn't know. My experience with brown trout over the years has produced all manner of colors and designs, including star shapes, but the differences occurred in different streams, with different feeding patterns. There didn't seem to be any divided genealogies in any one stream.

The next pool upstream produced another flash of gold, somewhat larger and cannier than the first. This fish was lying at the tail of a riffle, in shallow water, and at the sting of the hook immediately headed for a submerged bush. Burrowing into the leaves, he looked for a snag, apparently having been hooked before, perhaps a number of times. The bend of my rod finally generated enough pressure to pull the hook free, and he disappeared in a flurry of twigs and leaves.

This particular visit was on a sixty-degree day in December, in fact two weeks before Christmas. There was not a soul on the stream besides me, and I saw not even a boot print, but plenty of insect life was flying. Winter fishing conditions are the real beauty of trout angling in these southern Appalachians, and for some it's the best season. At the season's beginning, the road to the generating plant is one long parking lot, with people queuing up at their favorite holes. In December the Dan is an exclusive one-man club, shared with pods of friendly browns, rainbows, and brookies.

The rule of following streams up to their source until it hurts is particularly rewarding on the Dan. From the power plant to the first dam is a comparatively easy two-mile hike. Between the lower dam, Towne, and the upper dam, Talbott, high on the side of the Pinnacles of Dan, the going gets harder, with over five miles of excellent wild brook and rainbow fishing high up on the side of the Pinnacles, alluring enough to keep an absorbed angler stalking fish until dark through some difficult going. There are often plentiful midges over the water, and switching to a Number 18 Black Wulff sometimes proves a good choice.

Directions: On the Blue Ridge Parkway, just south of Meadows of Dan, turn south at milepost 184 onto VA(s) 614. Follow it through Bell Spur to VA(s) 631, turning left there. Route 631 becomes a gravel road leading to VA(s) 648, which is paved. Turn left on 648, and you will see the stocking signs along the Dan River. Stay on 648 until it dead-ends at the generating plant where written permission to fish must be obtained. From there up the Pinnacles of Dan access is by footpath only.

JENNINGS CREEK

STREAM TYPE: Freestone • USGS Arnold Valley • DeLorme 43, 53

One of the larger Virginia streams, the Jennings has one advantage, or disadvantage, depending upon your viewpoint. It closely follows VA(s) 614, a paved road well known to local fishermen. In fact they can look out of the front window of the Arcadia General Store across the road and see if the fish are rising. The store is also a Trout

Information Center for stocking alerts, road directions, and tips on what they're hitting. It's not a good idea to be standing near the front door if a stocking truck goes by, as you may be stampeded by beefy anglers in camouflage clothes.

But later in the season, when bass are fishable, the Jennings quiets down and becomes less of a put-and-take affair and more of a fly-fisherman's domain. The proximity of the James River, into which the Jennings flows, somewhat filters out the bass-fishing crowd in June and July, and that's really the time to see this stream at its best. Because of the meadows along its banks, floating hoppers may do well during warm-weather months. Toward dusk, a Number 8 or 10 white moth may snag one of the citation browns for which the Jennings is famous. For rising fish the smaller size standard patterns may be selected. Choose among Coachman, Adams, Light Cahill, Hendrickson, Blue Quill, Gray Fox, and Yellow Stonefly, depending upon the hatch.

So far we have been talking about the lower reaches of this stream. Upstream in the Jefferson National Forest, the Jennings becomes somewhat less of a social scene and more of a typical Appalachian spring creek. Its stream of origin is Fallingwater Creek, which aptly describes the terrain. Here it is possible to catch some small but energetic rainbow trout on black ants, nymphs, or a Number 14 dry beetle.

Because of its multiple personality, the Jennings is a good candidate all season long. If the banks down in Arcadia are too crowded early in the season, you can just move higher up into the mountains and have the fishing all to yourself on the Jennings or its regulated tributary, North Creek.

In the fall when the post-summer water temperature drops, downstream becomes the place to catch larger fish. And so far Virginia trout anglers are not taking full advantage of fall and winter fishing on the Jennings, which can be excellent at times.

Directions: Take Exit 48 off I-81 and follow VA(s) 614 to Arcadia. On the way you will cross a new concrete bridge which spans the James River. A reliable local landmark is the Arcadia General Store.

NORTH CREEK

STREAM TYPE: Freestone • USGS Arnold Valley • DeLORME 53

One frequent customer of the Orvis store in Roanoke, Virginia, fishes only North Creek, out of all the waters available to him. And a select number of other Old Dominion trout anglers have been heard to share this sentiment. Even a casual first look at this gemlike mountain stream hints that there is something special which attracts lovers of good trout water again and again.

Flowing through the Botetourt County section of Jefferson National Forest, North Creek tumbles through a mixture of hardwoods and hemlock. Every couple of hundred yards a freshet of spring water hits the main channel, forming small but deep pools. Each stretch affords another fishing opportunity, plus a new delight to the eye. The abundance of spring water and shade keeps North Creek ideally cool for trout even during midsummer. The mile-long regulated stretch is unstocked, and all the mostly wild rainbows reproduce naturally, fighting like the natives they really have become. Typically soft acid water, North Creek is better habitat for brook trout than for the other species.

Healthy mayfly hatches may be observed rising from the pools, particularly Sulfur Duns with spinners. A Number 16 imitation of this hatch can be productive. Since this is a steep-gradient forest stream, dry-fly-fishing is limited to short stretches of smooth water. Any of a selection of smaller dark nymphs are less frustrating to fish, along with black ants and Wooly Worms. It would be a safe guess that 90 percent of the diet here is nymphs.

The bank is somewhat crowded with mature trees, rather than bushes, making the backcast difficult. It is necessary to glance over your shoulder prior to the backward flip, making sure there is an opening between tree trunks. Even then a great deal of time will be spent sitting on a mossy hemlock root tying on a new fly. But the scenery more than compensates for the lost ties, and you may even be tempted to munch on an early spring teaberry or two just to freshen your mouth.

It may seem paradoxical, but on this small stream as on many other highland Virginia fisheries, a longer rod is preferable to some of the small, whippy models. With an eight-footer you can extend your leader upstream between limbs to hover above just the right stretch of tailwater. In some places you can cast by bending a longer rod into an arc by pulling back on the fly between your thumb and forefinger (carefully), releasing it, and catapulting the fly into just the right spot. This technique can explore narrow enclaves passed up by other fishermen but not by trout.

Special Regulations: On the stretch of water just above the North Creek National Forest Campground and continuing for about a mile upstream, fishing is restricted to single-hook artificial lures; creel limit 2 fish at least 9 inches long per day; fishing must cease when creel limit is attained.

Directions: Take Exit 48 off I-81, and follow VA(s) 614 to Arcadia. The road follows the larger Jennings Creek, into which North Creek flows—also good trout-fishing although strictly put-and-take in the spring. It's always a good idea to stop at the Arcadia General Store and ask about the fishing, since the main clientele there are fishermen and wardens. About a mile past the store, a sign directs you left onto a gravel road leading to the North Creek Campground, and a regularly stocked section of the stream parallels the road here. This is an immaculately maintained stretch of North Creek, with frequent manmade weirs damming up smooth stretches of water.

Just upstream from the campground a sign indicates the mile of regulated section, and there are frequent parking pull-offs. The road ends abruptly with the Appalachian Trail taking over. The walk up the trail to Apple Orchard Falls is worth the effort, as above the falls you may have a plethora of small but feisty native brookies all to yourself.

ROANOKE RIVER

STREAM TYPE: Limestone • USGS Elliston • DeLORME 41, 42

The story of this stream is a marvel of reclamation rather than of angling excellence. Meandering through the edge of downtown Roanoke, it is far from one of Virginia's premier trout streams, but fifty years ago it was the color and consistency of liquid green soap, supporting a few hardy mudcats, carrying all the effluvia of an open sewer. Today anglers in chest waders fish in the shadow of Veteran's Stadium, catching stocked fish. Hypothetically, a surgeon in Roanoke's largest hospital could walk out of the emergency room entrance in waders and vest and be fishing in two minutes. Happy-faced kids can be seen in the spring walking up from Wasena Park with limits of rainbow. Upstream near the city of Salem, the river has an Avonlike quality with colonies of mallards waddling across grassy banks.

In order to fairly evaluate the Roanoke as a trout stream, one should drive north of Salem down US 11 past Shawsville. There the Roanoke completely changes character from a placid river to a tumbling mountain stream, with Bony's Run and Dark Run infusing it with cold spring water all year around. Most of it is bordered by private land, prominently marked with Posted signs. However, access to stretches of trout water along the South Fork may be identified by signs showing where stocking took place. Eventually in Floyd County the Roanoke becomes Purgatory Creek, no longer a river but now a series of falls, riffles, and small pools flowing down the side of Lick Ridge.

The relatively few designated fishing areas tend to be crowded early in the season. Later on in June and July you won't find quite as many boot tracks, and this is the time to try an assortment of nymphs, black ants, and streamers. Upstream of Shawsville dry flies are difficult to fish because of the predominant rapids, but an Adams Number 20 may be dapped in the occasional enclaves of quiet water.

Downstream near the city it's a different story, with bathtublike stretches hundreds of yards long for floating a fly. The trouble here is fishing pressure from Roanokers who can change after work and get in a couple of hours of angling before dark. Holding out are a few suspicious brown trout who ignore the bait and spinners, hiding under the bank until late twilight. Large white moths or mosquitos might lure one of these wily monsters out of hiding late in the evening, but it's far from a sure bet.

Directions: To reach the South Fork of the Roanoke River, from I-81 turn off at the Dixie Caverns exit. Follow US 11/460 south into Shawsville. At the Meadowbrook Retirement Home turn left on VA(s) 637, which follows the stream all the way to its source.

ROARING RUN

STREAM TYPE: Limestone • USGS Strom • DeLorme 52

This is a mountain stream just within the boundary of the Jefferson National Forest. A high-banked steep-gradient stream with cascades and potholes, Roaring Run invites wet-fly and nymph fishing.

The stream banks are steep rock walls covered for the most part with damp moss. Occasional bare pine roots serve as convenient grab bars for those in need of such assistance. Mostly the water consists of heavy current, deep pools, and infrequent quiet stretches where fish may be observed rising to mayfly hatches. The early hatch seems to be Light Cahill, with a few Olive Blue Dun flies. There are a variety of other aquatic insects flying about the stream as well, so turn over some stones to check the nymph population before making your choice of lure.

Be prepared for heavy fishing traffic on Roaring Run, since despite its unspoiled appearance, the stream is paralleled by a well-maintained gravel road. It is close to population centers, and its reputation as a trout-producer is well known by fishermen of the area. Frequent whole-kernel corn cans and empty salmon egg jars remind us of the job still remaining for Trout Unlimited and other concerned troutists.

There are still some old-timers around who can remember when Roaring Run was a wilderness stream, to be experienced by those hardy enough to pack in a tent, army cots, cast iron skillet, and enough bacon, eggs, and beans to accompany the week's catch of fat brook trout. That Roaring Run is gone and can never be more than a memory.

At the end of the gravel road there is a well-manicured picnic ground about a pre–Civil War iron furnace dating in fact back to 1838. It is possible, if you walk upstream far enough, to recapture a little of the wilderness which once surrounded Roaring Run. This upper stretch is barred to motorized traffic, which thins out the less hardy. It does take some walking through moderately difficult terrain to reach wild rainbow territory.

Because of the heavy concentration of humanity around the picnic area, it is recommended that one go downstream to sample the sights and sounds of lower Roaring Run, which is a picture-postcard stream. But walking upstream above the old furnace can provide the connoisseur of wild trout fishing the essence of that sport. The paths are increasingly less beaten down as you proceed upstream, so you might consider saving your serious fishing time for this area.

Directions: Turning off of US 220 onto VA(s) 615 takes you alongside Craig Creek, which empties into the James River at the intersection. Upstream you encounter Roaring Run crossing the road at VA(s) 621. The turnoff is well marked by a National Forest sign reading "Roaring Run." A short distance later state stocking signs mark the trees.

ROCK CASTLE CREEK

STREAM TYPE: Freestone • USGS Woolwine • DeLorme 25

Rock Castle Creek flows through red clay country in Patrick County, which adjoins Henry County. And like the fiery patriot and sworn foe of the constitution who once governed these hills and whose namesake the counties are, the Rock Castle is somewhat of a paradox and a mystery. It has all the attributes of a productive Virginia mountain stream: frequent spring creeks feeding in cold water, an average thirty-foot width of rapids with pools below, state stocking which indicates promising trout habitat, plenty of aquatic insect life, and a good gravel-and-sand bottom. So what's the paradox? In spite of a remoteness which eliminates the slick-worn paths decorated with boot tracks, the hatches go undisturbed and fish are not easily spotted.

One might still be tempted to say this is a put-and-take stream with bruising traffic on the weekends, but that doesn't really seem to be the case. Sure, there is some evidence of bait fishermen, but the Rock Castle is the type of habitat which should be able to withstand moderate pressure. There don't appear to be many mayflies, but there are prolific midges and terrestrials. One possible solution to the mystery is the abundance of minnows, snails, and other underwater life forms. Turning over stones produces a stonefly larva or two, but no mayfly nymphs.

As for wet flies, a Muddler Minnow can produce some strikes, but they appear to be rainbow fingerlings, six inches or less. Starting halfway down VA(s) 837 and working upstream takes you through some reasonably attractive water. Under the VA(s) 837 bridge the water becomes deeper, and just above it there is a natural dam with green water under the falls. Farther along you find a still stretch relatively free of foliage, where dry flies may be floated naturally near huge sycamore stumps.

Then the overhanging vegetation takes over, and you may hang your hook in a selection of maples, spicewood, rhododendron, sycamore, and other brush on every other backcast. Another distraction to the first-time fisherman is the "gold" shining on the bottom—fool's gold or iron pyrite, of course, but flashing in the sun the particles look more like high-grade ore than the real thing does. This is also iron country, as evidenced by the brick color of the streambed and water that has a slightly ferrous odor and appearance. These mineral characteristics also exist in neighboring streams, like the Smith River, which some call the top trout stream in Virginia.

Add another paradox: the farther upstream you fish, the deeper the water appears to be, probably due to the high banks channeling the stream more closely. Up the mountainside approaching the Blue Ridge Parkway, the sand-and-gravel bottom gives way to stone, channeling rapids into plunge pools holding small brook trout. But this part of the stream without a doubt also holds some wise old heavy-bodied rainbows, but it's going to take some careful checkmate planning to unravel their secrets and penetrate their hideouts, with rapid-fire changes of lure until the bug-of-the-day is finally served up.

It may take more than one visit to the Rock Castle to fully unravel its mysteries, but it's worth a return trip. Or better yet, first find that rare species, a fly-fisherman familiar with the stream who is also willing to speak of its secrets. He might even give away the existence of excellent wild trout fishing if you go upstream far enough. Good luck!

Directions: Exit the Blue Ridge Parkway at Tuggle Gap and take VA 8 South, turning left on VA(s) 678 just north of the village of Woolwine. This takes you to the stocked section of Rock Castle Creek. A right turn on VA(s) 837 brings you parallel to a rhododendron-bordered area of the stream and after half a mile a dead end.

RUNNETT BAG CREEK

STREAM TYPE: Freestone • USGS Endicott • DeLORME 26

Runnett Bag Creek is for the most part a gentle-gradient stream, averaging twenty feet in width. Even in the low-water months it maintains a fair volume. Because of a heavy overgrowth of brush it is advisable to wade the streambed rather than attempting to hike along the banks. There is a proliferation of terrestrials, including grasshoppers, crickets, spiders, and beetles. The stream bottom tends to silt over, however, and some of the more inviting holes heat up too much in the summer for holdover trout.

State trout-stocking signs show up after the road emerges from a heavily timbered area, and they continue for approximately two miles of the paved road. Access to the stream is through private lanes turning west off the highway. Where VA(s) 818 turns right off VA(s) 793 there is a wooden bridge with fairly deep water beneath it alive with minnows and larger coarse fish. A week or two after one of Virginia's unannounced stockings, here would be the best time to try some small patterns such as Adams or Coachman Number 14.

The Runnett Bag is one of those streams close to population centers which present some fishing in early spring and during Indian summer. A gentle gradient plus abundant fine sand on the bottom make it an unproductive warm-weather fishery for the most part. One exception is the series of rapids behind the Endicott Assembly Church where there is a fairly steep drop. Man-assisted dams spill into well-oxygenated pools below, holding whatever wild rainbows survive through the summer.

Along the dirt stretch of VA(s) 793 leading down from the Blue Ridge Parkway there is evidence of heavy timber cutting, which may explain why the Runnett Bag has a cloudy look even when there have been no recent rains. This is an unstocked area, and though little more than a rivulet, it holds a few natives which can be spotted scurrying for cover. All of this timbered area is private property, and care should be taken to obtain permission to fish.

A typical sight in Runnett Bag Valley is an older citizen wearing gallus overalls and a John Deere or Caterpillar hat, walking along the road. These are friendly people, eager to talk and ready to admit they were makers of illegal whisky back in Prohibition days. In fact, it is grudgingly recorded that Franklin County was the champion producer of moonshine even into the thirties. At one time during the twenties, records show it led all U.S. counties in its purchase of refined sugar by the ton.

The younger inhabitants have adopted to an alarming degree the easier and more lucrative growing of marijuana as a substitute for bootlegging. These pot farmers are not such friendly people, and one state trooper reports finding fishhooks suspended on monofilament at eye level above the trail in an area south of here. He spotted them in time. If you glimpse a clearing along the stream bank displaying clusters of cannabis's characteristic spear-shaped leaves, instant departure is advised, and the same is probably good advice to those fishing any remote area of the country nowadays.

Directions: Driving south of Roanoke on the Blue Ridge Parkway to just past Smart View Park, turn left on VA(s) 793. This takes you off the crest of the Blue Ridge Mountains, down a gravel road which parallels the stream and eventually leads to pavement.

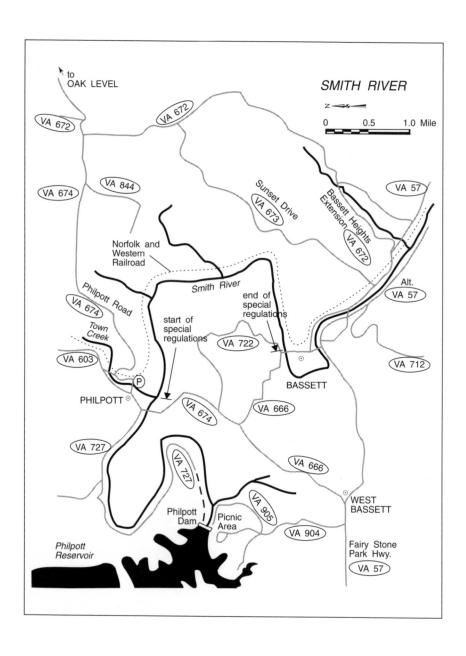

SMITH RIVER

STREAM TYPE: Freestone (lower tailwater)
USGS Bassett, Philpott Lake • DeLORME 26

In the unlikely event that Mother Nature and the Corps of Engineers were to collaborate on designing a fly-fishing stream, it would end up looking a lot like the Smith River. Its run-riffle-pool habitat is ideal for king-size browns, of which there is an abundance. The stream widens to over 100 feet in some places along the lower stretch. Although it's big water, hip waders will do fine, as shallow riffles frequently parallel deep pools on the opposite bank. There's enough gravel and sand to provide good footing almost everywhere.

The regulated stretch is vintage Appalachian, with flights of mallards tipping overhead and an occasional great blue heron grudgingly spreading its four-foot wings. Even in early spring, when the shadberry trees are starting to bloom, as many as four varieties of mayfly hatches may be observed, with midges and caddis thrown in just for the sake of confusion. It pays to take a good variety of flies along to the Smith, including various Cahills, some Number 18 Adams, Olive Midges, mosquitoes, and caddis. None of these are sure-fire, and it takes some casting to the rises to reveal which choice is best. Half the fun on this stream is matching the hatch. Once a choice is made for you by a big brown smacking the surface, the action comes fast and furious.

Occasionally the bucolic peace is ripped by the sound of a siren from Philpott Dam. When that happens, get out of the stream immediately, as a dangerous three-foot torrent of water soon follows. Information on water releases for power generation may be obtained by calling the U.S. Army Corps of Engineers at (703) 629-2432. Make it a point to check generating hours before traveling to the Smith. After a generating release stops, it may take an hour and a half for the water to subside to an ideal fishing level. The Corps of Engineers cooperates with fishermen on releases, although they caution that their release times are not absolutely accurate. Fishermen who resent the inconvenience of the water releases should reflect that without the cooling effect of water from the dam, this freestone stream would not be the brown trout fishery it is, particularly in midsummer.

With its alternating runs, riffles, and pools, the Smith River is ideal for king-size browns.

Much of the river bank displays rhododendron overhanging deep undercuts. Sizable trout may be seen feeding in these areas, presumably on terrestrials dropping from the branches. A black ant placed upstream to drift just under the rhododendron boughs can usually get a rise. These larger fish have seen just about every fly tied, so the smaller the pattern you show them, the better. And using a two-pound-test tippet may be worth all the fussy little twists and tangles it can produce.

The regulated portion of the Smith is a catch-and-release area, but there are enough sixteen-inch fish to make that a meaningful limit. One local fisherman marks off sixteen inches on his upper arm with a Magic Marker, saving the trouble of packing a ruler. This stream has developed quite a national reputation, and occasional license plates from Vermont or Wyoming can be seen. However far you have to travel, the mileage is worth the fun of a day's casting on the Smith. One aspect outsiders must get used to is the "gold" sprinkled along the river bottom. No matter how nuggetlike they may look, the "high-grade" particles always turn out to be pieces of mica reflecting gold from the sun, so you might as well concentrate upon the true gold reflecting from the sides of beautifully tinted brown trout.

In addition to the regulated section described here, there is excellent wild brown trout fishing all the way from the dam to Martinsville.

Special Regulations: Beginning just below the confluence of Town Creek and the Smith, and extending about 3 miles down to the VA(s) 666 bridge, fishing is restricted to single-hook artificial flies; creel limit 2 fish per day; all fish less than 16 inches long must be handled carefully and immediately returned unharmed to the water; possession of fish less than 16 inches long on this water is illegal; possession of bait on this water is illegal; fishing permitted year round.

Directions: Turn west off of US 220 at Oak Level. Follow VA(s) 674 all the way to the Norfolk and Southern Railway paralleling the river. One word of caution: just past Oak Level there is a right turn on 674 which looks like another road intersecting at 90 degrees and thus is very easy to miss. At the railroad crossing you may continue straight ahead to a parking area, or you may go left on a dirt road just before the tracks. This is a rough and rutty little road, almost a trail, but it gives best access for fishing the special-regulation area upstream.

6

New River Drainage Area

The New River is deceptively named, being the second oldest river in the world next to the Nile. Rising in western North Carolina, it runs northeast then north through Virginia, skirting the West Virginia border. At Gauley Bridge, West Virginia, it joins the Gauley River to form the Kanawha, which is part of the Ohio River watershed. It has the distinction of being the only surviving ancient river which rises in the Blue Ridge, cuts west through the mountains, and eventually supplies water to the Mississippi and the Gulf of Mexico. The icy water of its tributary the Little Stony, spilling over your hip waders, will eventually lap the shores of Veracruz.

The New shapes the look of the land surrounding it, in some areas being a flat half-mile across, dotted with anglers wading it knee-deep, spin fishing for redeyes. Winding back upon itself, the river dips between mountains and becomes narrow, deep walleye water. Free-stone streams like the regulated stretch of Little Stony Creek plunge down the mountainsides toward the New River gorges, pausing just long enough for prime mayfly hatches.

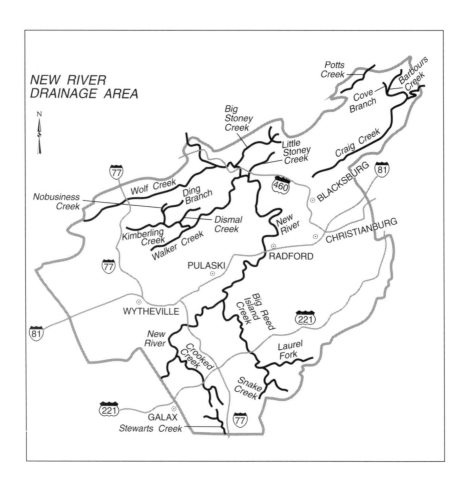

BARBOUR'S CREEK

STREAM TYPE: Freestone • USGS Newcastle • DELORME 52

All along VA(s) 617 Barbour's Creek is relatively small, with signs indicating it is stocked by the state. Farther upstream you enter what is called the National Forest Wilderness Area. Here the stream may be reached by a series of one-lane dirt forestry roads by going either right or left, as the stream crosses the highway frequently.

Above the Pines Campground and the Horse Corral, the stream

gradient becomes somewhat steeper, transforming Barbour's Creek into a series of small cascades with deep green grottoes beneath them. These deeper spots hold a number of trout hiding among the rocks at the stream bottom. The lower reaches offer wild brown and brook fishing, while the North Fork headwaters is strictly wild brook trout habitat.

Barbour's is one of the Craig County streams which enjoyed an early reputation as one of Virginia's finer trout fisheries. In recent years the stream has gone downhill somewhat due to overfishing plus habitat destruction by floods. The stream is still good trout habitat, however, and has the potential for restoration with more of the careful management it's receiving. Flies which do well here are Adams Number 14, Hare's Ear nymphs, Wulff patterns, and variations of the Coachman.

Directions: From Newcastle take VA(s) 615 to the east out of town. Turn left on VA(s) 609 until it dead-ends into VA(s) 611. At 611 one may go either left upstream or right downstream. The stream averages from fifteen to twenty feet wide and is relatively shallow. There are a couple of miles of private land, heavily posted. Turning right off of 611 onto 617, one eventually reaches the Jefferson National Forest campground called The Pines.

BIG STONY CREEK

STREAM TYPE: Freestone • USGS Lindside • DeLorme 41

Around the footbridge taking the Appalachian Trail across Big Stony, the terrain levels out appreciably. The rapids are consequently less swift and the holes not as deep. It is good trout water, with somewhat less pressure than the more scenic sections lower downstream. Because of the water's slower pace, there is a growth of algae on the streambed, and flat stones can be unavoidably slick, so choose your footing carefully and take advantage of the handholds afforded by overhanging rhododendron.

There is an excellent national forest campground at White Rocks, where leaders can be repaired, lunch eaten, or serious contemplation undertaken. There may be interruptions from the unruly population of red squirrels here, who specialize in peanut butter sandwich remnants.

Lower down, there are some quiet pools where rising fish may be spotted in midafternoon. A Number 18 or 20 Adams fly may prove effective. Hatches of Quill Gordons have been observed here in April.

Big Stony is one of Virginia's better-publicized streams, with nearly six miles of heavily fished water. Because of the nooks and crannies afforded by its big stones, it can hold fish despite the heavy early-season pressure. In addition to a good holdover population, the stream contains a fair number of wild browns and brooks. But these are lure-wary trout, requiring many selections of flies before the right combination is found. And some careful stalking behind the demanding rhododendron cover doesn't hurt either.

During Virginia's spring turkey season, a hunting break may be a pleasant midmorning distraction when the fishing slows down. Following feeder routes to the Appalachian Trail, you'll have only a short walk from the Big Stony to heavy turkey scratchings. One of the ironies of gobbler-hunting here is the likelihood of finding a truly virgin mountain spring creek. As one parts the laurel with a gun barrel, he may see a tiny stream's mirror surface broken by eight or ten native brookies of indeterminate size. And then, wouldn't you know, later in the afternoon the fishing may be interrupted by a couple of pterodactyl-size turkeys overhead cruising the stream.

Directions: Take I-81 south from Roanoke, follow Exit 37 at Christiansburg, and take US 460 west from Blacksburg. Passing through Pembroke, go 2 miles and take VA(s) 635 right. This road takes you into the Jefferson National Forest, where the signs indicate stocked water. Three miles upstream you enter an area lined with private cabins, but there is access for fishing here.

COVE BRANCH

Stream type: Freestone • USGS Potts Creek, Newcastle
DeLorme 52

Here's one of those streams which make you ask, "What am I doing here?" The water is totally dominated by the laurel bushes along the banks, which are steep enough to be approached with caution. You must ease the butt of your fly rod back through the laurel branches in order to reach the water with your fly. After hanging up half a dozen times, you wonder if the road to Cove Branch was the right one to take.

But then you begin catching wild brook trout which have seldom if ever before seen people, let alone a fly. There's a lack of pounded slick paths along the bank, an unfortunate characteristic of Virginia's more accessible stocked streams. And the stream is not blazed by a trail of soda bottles and beer cans. These brookies are truly natives.

Half the fun is getting there, up the forestry road, with deer and turkey to be seen during early-morning or late-evening hours. As you approach Cove Branch, you get the impression from the rushing noise that there's a formidable body of water there, but it's mostly a step-across stream. The undercut banks invite dapping a fly in the current, where wild trout are eager to leap after an Adams the second it hits the water.

Upstream from where the gravel road crosses Cove Branch at a bridge is the best fishing. Downstream for a short distance the stream is fishable, but then a single strand of barbed wire garnished with Posted signs lets you know this is private land.

Be prepared for greenbrier, since Cove Branch is the kind of stream for which it was invented. Be also aware that this stream is classified as borderline acidic by the state, and even though brook trout are more resistant to acid than rainbows, the fishing here could turn progressively sourer. In fact Cove Branch has recently been removed from the list of state-stocked streams.

Directions: Turn northeast off of VA 311 onto VA(s) 617. Turn left on VA(s) 611 for a mile, then right onto 617 again. From there turn left onto FR 176 and hold tightly to the steering wheel. There is an obscure sign directing you to Cove Branch, but it's better just to look

Lew Thurman, retired banker and noted maker of split-bamboo rods, fishing a limestone stream in Craig County.

for the stream crossing through culverts underneath FR 176. There's ample streamside parking just off the road on the right.

CRAIG CREEK

STREAM TYPE: Freestone • USGS McDonald's Mill • DeLorme 41

Anyone looking for beaucoup trout in plenty of water might as well stay away from the headwaters of Craig Creek. But the student of trout, interested in seeing a small display case of mountain-stream habitat, will be handsomely rewarded by this stream.

Local residents know Craig Creek as a bass fishery, with its wide, meadow-bordered waters inhabited by an assortment of pickerel, perch, and rough fish. This is the Craig County face of the stream. But across the Montgomery County line it assumes another identity altogether. Here in glassy little pools the microcosmic infant Craig Creek trickles along under massive rock cliffs and through laurel and rhododendron glens. This is one of those just-for-fun streams mostly shallower than your ankle bone. An occasional chest-deep pool will hold a family of five or six fourteen-inch holdover stocked trout gazing up with a disarming innocence. You can sit on a carpet of pine needles and observe them going about their daily business, mostly feeding on gnats, ants, and small beetles. Any movement on your part will cause mild alarm, sending the fish meandering to crevices in rocks and sunken logs.

Fishing this stretch of the stream is a matter of outwitting these small families of brookies and rainbows, wearing camouflage clothing, using natural cover, with plenty of 4X or smaller leader tied to Number 20 terrestrials. Success is directly proportional to patience, as once these trout see you above their glassy pool, there's little chance of their taking your fly. So be prepared for much slow and careful stalking behind natural cover.

It is to be hoped that all those fishing this pearl of a stream will realize what a delicate crucible of life it really is. These are amazing fish, heavy and healthy-looking, making the most of what food is available to them. Watching them go about their daily business affords a stream-side classroom in trout ecology, with water so clear you can see the bottom from fifty feet away. The experience gives one the feeling for how wild trout thrived in this country for millennia before there was need for a stocking program. It proves that a step-across brook really is capable of supporting decent-sized trout as long as human greed doesn't catch up with them. How many of these survivors you can catch is unimportant compared to how many you can release back into their small universe. We hope there are enough people around who like to see trout in a trout stream to conserve this family.

Directions: Take I-81 Exit 40A at Salem, go north on VA 311. Turn left on VA(s) 621, and follow it to the Craig / Montgomery County line. Proceed to a national forest area sign, Caldwell Fields, and go upstream about 2 miles from there. Trout-stocking signs are posted, but some of the more interesting dirt roads lead to unstocked areas.

CROOKED CREEK

STREAM TYPE: Freestone • USGS Woodlawn • DeLorme 24

The Crooked Creek Wildlife Management Area holds within its borders approximately seven miles of trout streams. The Virginia Department of Game and Inland Fisheries maintains holding tanks on the premises, from which the waters are stocked four days a week. This unique experiment by the state is a veritable supermarket of angling. You might say there is something here for trout anglers of every persuasion: quiet pools flowing through a meadow behind the parking lot; moderately riffled areas running through a small gorge, all heavily stocked; and for the fly-flickers, the best bet is the East Fork of Crooked Creek, an area of native brook trout only, no stocking. It is recommended you allot at least a full day to explore the fishing here. Two days would be even better.

Trout here run the gamut from native brooks, which fight like fish twice their size, through freshly stocked rainbows barely weaned off Purina Trout Chow, to eight-pound browns brooding for years in dark pockets beneath the banks. Since this is a game-management area as well as a managed fishery, fishermen are likely to see a king turkey gobbler and his harem drinking from the creek, or a herd of deer at twilight packed into a small mountain meadow. Frequently you will run across vacant cadavers of frame houses which once housed hardscrabble farmers and their families when it was possible for them to make a living in areas such as this.

To fish the east fork of Crooked Creek, drive to the holding tanks and park in a designated area. Then cross the stream and follow the right-hand fork to the dam. Next do some ridge-running a short distance upstream to the unstocked area, where privacy is guaranteed, except for some exceptionally feisty wild brookies.

This is vintage Appalachian stream fishing, with ten-foot canopies of rhododendron kissing the stream. Be prepared for your fly to catch on the branches and leaves of these attractive but unyielding bushes.

And another tip: don't try any cross-country shortcuts to another section of the stream.

The rhododendron jungle, rivaling any mangrove forest, stretches on for hundreds of acres of totally confusing maze. Stick to wading, and you'll avoid the crush.

This is a stream for small nymphs and streamers, cast a few feet up a fall and allowed to drift back down into the hole beneath. Take a good assortment of small terrestrials as well, and watch to see what's dropping off the overhang. A Number 18 black ant can be dapped from an eight-foot rod on just ten or so feet of line out, with a good concealing boulder in front of you. Moderately good hatches of Dark Cahills have been seen emerging on the East Fork, with plenty of winged ants clambering over the boulders.

Frankly, these fish, like all natives, are fickle. If they don't choose to feed at your designated time, forget it. No amount of fly-changing or streamside tying to match the hatch will be effective. They will follow your fly in droves and inevitably turn away at the last moment. And just as suddenly they will start feeding, striking nearly everything.

Special Regulations: Crooked Creek and its tributaries are fee-fishing water: a daily permit costing $3.50 is required in addition to a Virginia fishing license. The permit can be obtained at the refreshment area and must be signed by the licensee. Creel limit 5 trout per day; season runs from 9:00 A.M. on the first Saturday in March through January 31 (note: fee permit not required after Labor Day, although a Virginia trout stamp is); daily fishing hours are 7:00 A.M. to 6:00 P.M. in March and April, and 6:30 A.M. to 7:00 P.M. May through September.

Directions: From I-81, turn south onto I-77 and follow that to the Hillsville exit. Get on US 221 south for 8 miles to VA(s) 620, and turn right to reach the East Fork. This is a small county road which dribbles away into a dirt lane. Don't become discouraged, as along the way there are prominent road signs showing the way to Crooked Creek. For those more leisurely travelers following the Blue Ridge Parkway, take the Meadows of Dan exit for US 58 north to Hillsville. Then turn south on US 221 and follow the above directions.

DISMAL CREEK

STREAM TYPE: Freestone • USGS Mechanicsburg • DeLORME 40

It's not too difficult to imagine a cartographer at the turn of the nineteenth century suddenly coming upon a stream in the "deep woods." Perhaps the November wind is whipping a few snowflakes onto the water, and it's getting dark enough to make camp. Unrolling his parchment, this buckskin-clad place-namer wrote "Creek" next to the meandering stream line he had just drawn. Pondering for a moment while looking at the dark bellies of early-winter clouds, he added "Dismal." To all those travelers who followed his map, headed west on the Wilderness Road, this stream was "The Dismal." And so it remains to this day.

On a spring morning when the sunlight is just beginning to dance off its riffles, the last word any trout-seeker of today would use to describe this stream is dismal—"delightful," perhaps; or "distracting," but never dismal. On the opposite bank there is an occasional glimpse of the Appalachian Trail, which may be reached by a log bridge. The quiet might be broken by a grouse exploded from the greenbriers by the unnatural flapping of hip waders.

This lower stretch is deep and rapid, with healthy trout favoring undercut holes beside the bank. If you're fishing from midstream, casts can be directed to the right or left with equal success. This is a wet-fly stream, although the chorus of dry-fly purists may disagree. Start with a March Brown Number 10, or a Light Cahill Number 14 nymph, depending upon what is clinging to the stones. Take some time to observe which edible insects are dropping from the overhanging vegetation. Sometimes changing to a shiny green beetle can whet a big brown's appetite. A Hare's Ear offers some variety when none of these are working for you.

Above the falls there is a dense wall of laurel and greenbriers intermingled, with glassy-slick rocks underfoot. There are holdover fish here, no doubt because of the impossible casting conditions; you find yourself hanging on to a laurel limb and trying to find a hole large enough even to accommodate your rod tip. This *could* get dismal.

A better idea would be to bypass the wall of vegetation by driving

Steve and Tammy Hiner collect insects on a Craig County stream.

upstream to the White Pine Horse Camp where a smaller but more inviting version of the stream beckons. Here there is open country, much more sunlight reaching the water, and the possibility of finding a hatch of Green Drakes or maybe some terrestrials such as black jassids or flying ants. Large stretches of the Dismal do dry up during periods of extreme drought.

This corner of the Jefferson National Forest is also home to virtually unknown little trout havens such as Nobusiness Creek or Ding Branch—worth exploring although not worth a detailed description in this book. Checking a map of the local area will reveal a rich network of these small branches, not necessarily tributaries of Dismal Creek.

Directions: From I-81 take Exit 32 onto VA 100 north past Dublin. From 100 turn west (left) onto VA 42 near Poplar Hill. Follow 42 through White Gate to VA(s) 606, and turn north (right). You will cross Dismal Creek at the sawmill on the left, and take the next right, following the Dismal upstream. A dirt road turns off and dead-ends at Dismal Falls, where your vehicle may be parked.

HELTON CREEK

STREAM TYPE: Freestone • USGS Whitetop Mountain
DeLorme 22, 23

Helton Creek is a moderately small but picturesque stream, stocked at the lower end. Above the Upper Helton Baptist Church it's surrounded by private property, although no Posted signs are apparent. One small corner of Jefferson National Forest crosses it here. Despite the frequency of small farms, Helton Creek preserves its identity pretty well. Higher up, it narrows to about half its downstream size, becoming a native trout habitat.

Lower down where the Helton is markedly wider, it also drops at a steeper gradient. Boulders in the streambed are smaller than in other local streams and therefore don't offer the angler as much cover. In the steeper portion there are a number of pools, but none of these appears to be over six feet deep.

This stream is the type one might include as a summertime side trip when action on the nearby Whitetop Laurel or Big Wilson slows down. The lower temperature of its headwaters may provide action when warmer pools on the large streams do not.

Directions: From I-81 take Exit 16 onto VA 16 south. At the intersection at Volney, take VA 58 west, past Grayson Highlands State

Park, to VA(s) 783, a dirt road turning off to the right and following Helton Creek to its source.

LAUREL FORK (CARROLL COUNTY)

Stream type: Freestone • USGS Laurel Fork • DeLorme 25

Just when you had finished your list of favorite Virginia trout streams, along comes a sleeper like Laurel Fork, and immediately becomes one of your top ten. It takes some exploring, with many unnumbered dirt roads along the way, many of them dead ends. But the angling reward is well worth the gasoline expended.

Laurel Fork is a beautiful stream, and large as Virginia trout waters go, averaging seventy-five feet across, downstream from the village of Laurel Fork. Its abundant flow comes from frequent feeder streams, cooling the water in summer. It has stretches of relatively slow rapids, most of which are deep enough to hold trout well. It's not the sort of mountain stream which has falls with deep holes beneath, but rather follows a gentle gradient with riffles followed by flat rapids.

There is a modest population of wild browns and brooks here, with stocked rainbows only. The rainbows are hefty fish, running a foot or larger in length, with deep, heavy bodies. There is evidence of spawning activity, boding well for the holdover population. Fish have been observed in late autumn feeding upon hoppers and unidentified large-winged terrestrials. The Muddler Minnow was effective dropped into the rapids and allowed to drift into backwater pools.

A few miles away is Burk's Fork, prominently visible from the roads leading to Laurel Fork and similar to that stream. Burk's Fork is not listed separately in this book because all access appears to be from the shoulder of paved roadway, except where the land is heavily posted. There may be convenient public access somewhere, but it is not readily apparent.

There are signs of heavy fishing on Laurel Fork at the end of the more hidden access roads, as might be expected, since there are so few of them. On the other hand there are long stretches of stream along the paved county roads, such as VA(s) 630. The stream is somewhat abused here, with dumping and an occasional submerged tire. One would do well to move upstream from the roads and explore the more obscure stretches of Laurel Fork.

Of course, there are no barely touched trout streams in the eastern United States, although the closest you can approach them is in Virginia's Appalachians. No matter how far upstream you wade Laurel Fork, the tips of overhanging rhododendron limbs have been stripped bare of leaves, mementos of anglers grabbing for stability while navigating occasional slippery rock ledges. Fortunately, there are stretches of gravel, making for less-demanding wading, and even among the ledges, strips of gravel provide a foothold for dunk-free casting.

Directions: From the Blue Ridge Parkway, take the Meadows of Dan exit to VA 58 west to the village of Laurel Fork. Turn right onto County Road 638, following it several miles to where VA(s) 628 turns to the left and parallels Burk's Fork. Take another left at VA(s) 660, following it south to VA(s) 664, turning right there and following 664 for half a mile. Then take VA(s) 661 to the left, follow it half a mile—and here's where it gets tricky.

VA(s) 661, which is a dirt road, turns ninety degrees to the right at a row of mailboxes. Do *not* follow the turn, but instead go straight ahead onto a small unmarked country lane. This gradually narrows to a two-track overhung with small trees, leading downward toward the streambed. It sounds worse than it is, and does not require four-wheel-drive when dry, although the last couple of hundred yards requires bouncing from rock to rock. It dead-ends at streamside, next to the remains of a swinging bridge, and this is still public roadway with parking no problem as long as you do not block access to the summer cabins to the right and left. This was once a ford, but one look at the opposite bank affirms that Hurricane Hugo has barricaded the road with an impossible maze of blowdowns. Fishing is excellent both up and downstream from the former ford.

The key to gaining access to Laurel Fork is explore, explore, explore, as it does not pass through any public land. The route described above leads to a relatively private stretch of stream, but some nosing about will undoubtedly lead to equally good access.

Harry Steeves about to land a native brookie on his favorite stream, Little Stony.

LITTLE STONY CREEK

Stream type: Freestone • USGS Eggleston • DeLorme 41

The Little Stony is one of those good news–bad news streams which portend the future of trout fishing in the state of Virginia. Most of the news is good. This is a regulated stream, single-hook artificial lures only. It is not stocked, and manages to maintain a good population of both rainbow and brook trout.

In the early forties the Little Stony was stocked with rainbows, the stocking "took," and its descendants are still around. One piece of good news is that the brook trout have managed to coexist with their more aggressive rainbow neighbors, which does not always happen. The Little Stony is also lucky enough to have been chosen by Trout Unlimited for its brand of enlightened attention.

So what's the bad news? Perhaps the worst of it is apathy—meaning there are "power bait" anglers who occasionally take advantage of the Little Stony's fragile ecology. Probably the worst news is that there aren't more regulated Little Stonys around the state. We hope that will change.

If someone had said, "We're going to design the model Appalachian trout stream. First of all, it must be crystal clear and pure, with nothing around it but national forest. Second, it must have cascades with deep green holes below. Third, it must be scenic, with hemlocks, laurel, wildflowers, and a few mossy boulders scattered around. And fourth, there must be a good variety of aquatic insects, particularly caddis flies and midges, but with a good cross section of mayflies." The result of all this would have been the Little Stony.

As you cross the Little Stony's lower footbridge, the first thing which strikes your eye is a pod of rainbows lying beneath the rippled surface. Backlit with an amber light from somewhere, the underwater rock ledges frame the twelve- to fourteen-inch fish. Most of the Trout Unlimited people who come here bypass these showcase fish and head upstream.

As one TU member said, "I start out on the Little Stony by just sitting down in the water, because it's certainly going to happen to me anyway." Maybe an exaggeration, but there's no doubt about the slickness of these rocks; and when you add in the heavy current dropping down the mountainside, a wading staff can be a friend indeed. Contrary to the usual pattern, the holes get deeper and wider as you fish upstream, probably because the steeper gradient there causes the water to churn away more of the streambed.

There are walking trails on both banks of the stream, placed there by the Jefferson National Forest Commission, which maintains them regularly. Many people come just to walk the trail to the cascades, where another footbridge crosses. Above the cascades there is some trout activity, but you soon hit private land. The rainbows take caddis flies and light mayfly ties, but also slam a floating black ant cast into the rapids. There's abundant overhanging laurel, rhododendron, and hemlock, so be prepared for much patient untangling and unhooking from the vegetation.

This is challenging terrain and calls for an experienced fly-fisherman to take full advantage of its charms. It's not the sort of stream to which you would take a new bride for her first fly-casting lessons. Casts may be short, with a quick retrieve to keep the line from bellying. This rapid casting pattern combined with maintaining your footing in slippery-rock rapids, makes the Little Stony a physically demanding day's workout. But with the right fly patterns and a little skill, you'll catch decent-sized fish here for a stream this small. So you take a pratfall or two in the icy water—it's more than well worth it!

Directions: From I-81 take Exit 37 at Christiansburg to Bypass US 460 west. Follow Bypass US 460 and US 460 through the town of Pembroke, where a national forest sign indicates the Cascades (not to be confused with the Cascades at the Homestead). Turn right here onto VA(s) 623, which takes you to a parking area just below the regulated fishing. Don't be confused by other Little Stony Creeks, as there are many duplications of names in Virginia. These were isolated settlements at the time the streams were christened, and the surveyors just wrote on their maps any name which seemed to fit the milieu.

POTTS CREEK

Stream type: Limestone • USGS Potts Creek • DeLorme 40, 52

A large stream by Virginia mountain standards, Potts Creek has an abundance of terrestrials and some productive mayfly hatches, Green Drake and Sulfur Duns in particular. From the steel bridge downstream this is considered mainly a bass fishery, although some large trout hang at the junctions of small feeder streams, of which there are many. When there is a mayfly hatch below the Steel Bridge Campground, casting to a rise will almost invariably produce a rock bass or a feisty smallmouth. The prime trout water is upstream from the campground, with deep holes and some of the slickest rocks you'll find. At the steel bridge there is a slate bottom, with knife edges which give good traction but are unkind to the hands if you should fall. Above and below this slate area is a reddish Catawba stone bottom with a surface resembling glass.

These trout are large, and they're wily in June from the heavy fishing pressure they received early in the season. The waters tend to warm up later in the summer, so it's best to visit Potts Creek before the July heat sets in. Traveling the bank is not recommended, as there is a proliferation of greenbrier, designed to cause misery to mankind, grabbing landing nets or tearing new buttonholes in designer clothes. It's best to stay with the streambed.

This stream is stocked regularly, and is one of the more productive Virginia fisheries. An article in the Roanoke newspaper tells of a local fisherman taking 112 trout in a day from one elongated rock-bed pool. The story continues that these were freshly stocked fish, taken by jigging two-inch minnows. Using this method, the gentleman caught a total of 734 trout in the spring of 1990. That's the down side of the story. The up side is that he is not a keeper, and all fish were returned to Potts Creek mainly unharmed. The other upbeat note is that there are plenty of trout, some of them uncommonly large, in this stream. Using a weighted Muddler Minnow, the fly-fisherman can replicate this number-cruncher's experience.

Directions: Take US 311 from Exit 40A off I-81 at Salem and go north to Paint Bank. From the state trout hatchery proceed to the bottom of the mountain and take VA(s) 18 to the right, which is 18 north. Continue to the Steel Bridge Campground, maintained by the U.S. Forest Service.

SNAKE CREEK

STREAM TYPE: Freestone • USGS Fancy Gap • DeLORME 25

Here's an angling enigma. This stream has been described in a state publication as having a fair population of native brook trout plus a holdover of stocked fish. And yet a look at the Snake along VA(s) 922 reveals a largely silted bottom—the stream is dammed by beavers at several points—and little evidence of trout. There is a bounty of insect life over the stream, and yet no surface feeding. The beavers have worked this stream so industriously that there are even partly gnawed trees wrapped in fence wire to protect them from further incising. Beaver damming can help the trout habitat of some fisheries, but the property along Snake Creek is so heavily grazed that these dams only cause the silt to accumulate even more alarmingly.

The Big Snake is around eighteen feet wide in the special-regulations areas, with a good flow of water, following a slight gradient downstream. There are no plunge pools or rapids of any significance. It is stocked periodically with fish eight to ten inches in length.

With a lot of cooperation from landowners and intensive management by the Virginia Department of Game and Inland Fisheries, Snake Creek has the potential of becoming a four-star brown trout fishery. It's far from being there at this time, however, and may take years to develop fully.

Steve Hiner working Stewart's Creek one 47-degree December morning.

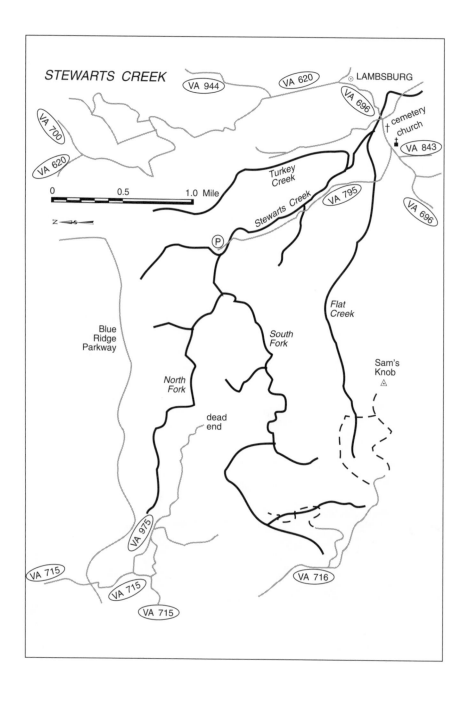

Special Regulations: On Big Snake Creek below Hill Ford and on Little Snake below the junction of VA(s) 922 and 674, fishing is restricted to single-hook artificial lures; creel limit 6 fish at least 12 inches long.

Directions: Turn east off I-77 at Hillsville onto VA 58. At Red Hill turn right onto VA(s) 674. Then turn left on VA(s) 922, which follows the special-regulations section of Snake Creek.

STEWART'S CREEK

STREAM TYPE: Freestone • USGS Lambsburg • DELORME 24

Stewart's Creek is still a heavily pressured stream, though it has been converted to a catch-and-release trout fishery. Nevertheless, it is holding its own as a prolific stream. One angler counted over 100 strikes in a day, mostly small fish, and mostly missed due to early-season rustiness. It's a high-gradient freestone stream with a dense riparian canopy, mostly rhododendron. Surrounded by over 1,000 acres of the Stewart's Creek Wildlife Management Area owned by the state, it flows for around 4½ miles, including the North and South forks.

The State of Virginia purchased this property in 1987 just in time to save Stewart's Creek from degradation due to poor logging practices. The erosion has been checked by stabilizing exposed soil through some pretty imaginative measures. What were once raw banks are covered with attractive greenery, and the waters are sparkling clear.

The lower stretch is good for a fair number of small, scrappy brook trout, which may be easily seen darting over the gravel-and-stone bottom. Farther upstream the gradient becomes much steeper, with plunge pools around every fifty feet, still averaging ten feet in width. The brookies are larger here, and as plentiful as one would think in a catch-and-release environment where only single-hook artificial lures are permitted.

The farther up the mountain you go, the steeper and more interesting Stewart's gets. From 100 feet up on the vertical slope, you can occasionally spot a sizable trout. The trick then is to lower yourself down the bank slowly and carefully enough not to scare him, and drop your Adams Number 16 upstream in front of his nose. If he gulps it, you are then dazzled by brilliant scarlet flashes as he porpoises around the pool.

In addition to using attractor flies such as the Adams, you may find it possible to match an assortment of mayfly hatches rising throughout the year. Even in mid-December some Olive Quill nymphs and mature stoneflies are in evidence, along with the usual midges inevitably appearing around midday.

AUTHOR'S NOTE: My normally reliable minnow imitations, such as a weighted Muddler, appeared to hold no attraction for the Stewart's feeders on a day when the water temperature measured 47 degrees at 11:00 A.M. On this mid-December day the ambient temperature was above 60 degrees, so the water warmed up even more later in the afternoon. There are no absolutes on these native trout streams, and a premeditated "cookbook" approach simply doesn't work. But that's what keeps it interesting.

On the South Fork, there is a last upper stretch of source water which leads almost vertically up the north slope of Sam's Knob. More demanding for the angler than the lower stretches, it may be the last habitat for generations of native trout which escaped the past century's logging operations. A more civilized route to this upper stretch heads down from above, leading off the Blue Ridge Parkway onto VA(s) 715. Then take a left onto VA(s) 975, at the Stewart's Creek Wildlife Management Area sign. This leads in slightly over a mile to a dead end at the North Fork.

Directions: Take I-77 south past Hillsville and across the Blue Ridge Parkway. Exit on VA(s) 620 to the west through Lambsburg, where you turn left onto VA(s) 696. After a short distance, turn right onto VA(s) 795, which leads into the Stewart's Creek Wildlife Management Area. The road dead-ends beside the stream in a parking area.

7

Mount Rogers
National Recreation Area

Driving out VA 58 toward the Whitetop Laurel, a newcomer may try to catch a glimpse of Mount Rogers, at 5,729 feet Virginia's highest. But there are no Wyoming Rockies here, thrusting above the horizon. These are old mountains, and Rogers is a round-shouldered giant hidden behind a rampart of wooded foothills. To the southwest is Whitetop Mountain, 5,540 feet, and Pine Mountain, 5,526 feet, all within the 154,000-acre Mount Rogers Recreation Area, most of which is included in the Jefferson National Forest.

The three wilderness areas here are Lewis Fork, 5,730 acres, Little Dry Run, 3,400 acres, and Little Wilson Creek, 3,855, adjacent to Grayson Highlands State Park. Little Wilson is the one of most interest to anglers, with a native trout fishery which wanders between alpine meadows down to Wilson Creek.

This section of the state, sometimes called the Virginia Highlands, is a gem of many facets. If you like your spring trout fishing among cascades of purple rhododendron or banks of pink and white laurel, this is the place to come in April. You run the risk of having your eye distracted away from your floating Adams by the dazzling scene around every bend in the stream.

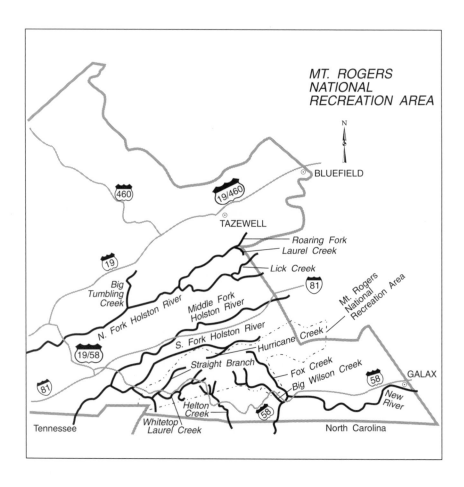

BIG TUMBLING

STREAM TYPE: Freestone • USGS Saltville • DELORME 22

What strikes you most when you enter the Big Tumbling Gorge is the perpetual twilight, even at midmorning on a July day. It's cool, dim, and steep, with the stream living up to its name by rolling noisily from the top of Clinch Mountain. How steep? Well, steep enough that the fish-management people stock the stream by cable, lowering containers of fish on pulleys into pools at the foot of stair-step rapids. Stocking takes place every day except Sunday. At the headwaters, on the mountaintop, Laurel Bed Lake is stocked in November with as many as 8,000 brook trout and 3,000 rainbows.

Sure, this is a fee-fishing stream, but angling here is anything but easy. Thigh muscles will get a workout, and much of your travel time may be spent clinging to branches hanging over the steep banks. Because of the dim light imposed by overhanging bowers of hemlock and oak, light-colored dry flies work well: Light Cahill Number 12 and white moths, for example. Muddler Minnow Number 12's with metallic and red enhancement are recommended in deep pools beneath falls and rapids. These are sizable and healthy fish, many of them holdovers, and they show a lot of fight in the relatively small Big Tumbling pools.

Special Regulations: Big Tumbling is fee-fishing water: a daily permit costing $3.50 is required in addition to a Virginia fishing license. The permit can be obtained at the refreshment area; special trout license not required. The water is closed to fishing each evening at specified times depending on the hour of sunset; fishermen are advised to confirm the closing time, for there is a $40 fine for fishing when the stream is closed.

Directions: From I-81 take Exit 13, following VA 107 through Chilhowie north to Saltville. Turn left on VA 91 at Saltville, then, within 0.5 mile, right on VA(s) 634 to Allison's Gap, left on VA(s) 613, and right on VA(s) 747. Look for signs reading "Clinch Mountain Wildlife Management Area."

BIG WILSON CREEK

STREAM TYPE: Freestone • USGS Troutdale • DeLorme 23

Big Wilson is typical of rhododendron-lined streams in the Virginia Highlands area. From the road, its waters seem lost at times in the maze of trailer-sized boulders. These give the angler a screen for approaching pools unseen, and provide pockets for trout protection. Walking down to streamside, you see a healthy small-stone-and-pebble bottom, abundant water from mountain spring branches, and stair-steps of falls and pools at frequent intervals. Almost every pool harbors at least one small holdover rainbow well into winter.

Higher on the mountainside, the stream, appropriately labeled Big Wilson down to the village called Mouth of Wilson, is just plain Wilson Creek. As you proceed upstream, the state stocking signs run out, along with the beaten paths and litter. As the stream narrows, it becomes classic native trout water. Above two summer cabins the road becomes more of a series of semi-level boulder tops, requiring four-wheel drive—difficult access but worth it.

Stoneflies are an important item in the diet of Big Wilson trout, as in other streams around the Mount Rogers area. The five key stonefly species provide both spring and winter hatches. A genus of giant stonefly, *Pteronarcys,* is common here, and may be imitated in its nymph stage with a giant black stone nymph pattern, which makes a hefty mouthful. For more picky eaters, the Little Yellow Stonefly is particularly prevalent in these freestone headwaters from May to July. Among other mayflies, Green Drakes emerge abundantly in May here and in the other Mount Rogers streams.

The overhanging vegetation makes terrestrials a consideration as well. There are times when only beetles and ants are taken near the Wilson's banks, while midstream trout are feeding on some form of aquatic insects.

Directions: From I-81, take Exit 16 onto VA 16 south to Volney. Proceed to the intersection, and take VA 58 West. Where Wilson Creek crosses under a bridge, take VA(s) 817, a dirt road that traces the Big Wilson to its source.

FOX CREEK

STREAM TYPE: Freestone • USGS Troutdale • DeLorme 23

Fox Creek is one of those on-again, off-again conservation stories all too familiar to those who like to see trout restored to a classic stream. At the beginning of this century, Grayson County's Fairwood Valley was a showplace of all the best of the Virginia Highlands. Virgin spruce

Floating a midge under a fallen tree on a Mount Rogers stream.

and hemlock completed their life cycles as they had for thousands of years, and Fox Creek brimmed with brook trout.

The industrial revolution in Grayson County took the form of Shay locomotives chuffing up the mountainsides and carrying away the heritage of the "Deep Woods," as Virginia was once called. Even with muscle and crosscut saws, it only took a very few years to level the forest, leaving the land ravished and the soil unprotected. Cattle cropped what little streamside vegetation remained, topsoil washed away, and fires ran through the dry slash left by loggers. Nevertheless, in spite of average water temperatures around 78 degrees, the maximum survival limit of rainbow trout, a few hardy fish remained. The brookies long ago retreated upstream to Lewis Fork, a small feeder at the headwaters. Then in the early 1980s the Virginia Department of Game and Inland Fisheries selected Fox Creek as a model of stream rehabilitation. In 1983 the first log channel constrictors and dams were set in place. But it wasn't until 1987 that the cattle standing in Fox Creek, blissfully unaware of the damage they were causing, were barred from the stream by fences complete with turnstiles for fisher-men. Since then some 3,400 trout have been placed in the stream annually, with the hope that eventually wild trout will reproduce in the improved habitat.

The streamside vegetation proliferated, cutting down the "limit-out" bait-fishing crowd and leaving room for fly-fishermen. The rainbow population grew steadily. Then in the fall of 1989 Hurricane Hugo struck, carrying away fences and K-dams, and fanning out the mica-laden soil back into flat stretches which heat up past trout survival limits. Since then the cooperative effort between the U.S. Forest Service and the Virginia Department of Inland Fisheries to rehabilitate the stream continues and is strongly supported by the work of individual trout fishermen. A lot of sweat and funding has gone into overcoming the abuse of Fox Creek and restoring it as a valuable cold-water fishery. It's holding rainbow trout, but the hurricane's effects will take some years to overcome.

A visit to Fox Creek is worth it—for the fishing, but also to observe trout conservation at its best. At this point the only element strongly lacking is an area restricted to artificial, single-hook lures along the most critical mile-and-a-half stretch. The Fox can be fished for many miles below the regulated area, with some excellent spots worth exploring. This is mostly private land, and permission from owners should be obtained. If you fish Fox Creek, fish it gently, and remember that every rainbow you release may become a parent.

Directions: From I-81 take Exit 16 onto VA 16 south, and continue to Troutdale. Turn west (right) there onto VA(s) 603 to Fairwood, center of the Fox Creek Restoration Area.

HOLSTON RIVER, SOUTH FORK

STREAM TYPE: Limestone • USGS Marion • DeLORME 22, 23

As you follow the South Holston past Buller Fish Cultural Station, it's worth a stop to take a look at the muskies raised there. Although the main product of the fishery is bass, you'll probably find at least one toothy monster three feet long, staring unblinkingly with crocodile eyes. These are not what you came for, though they are stocked

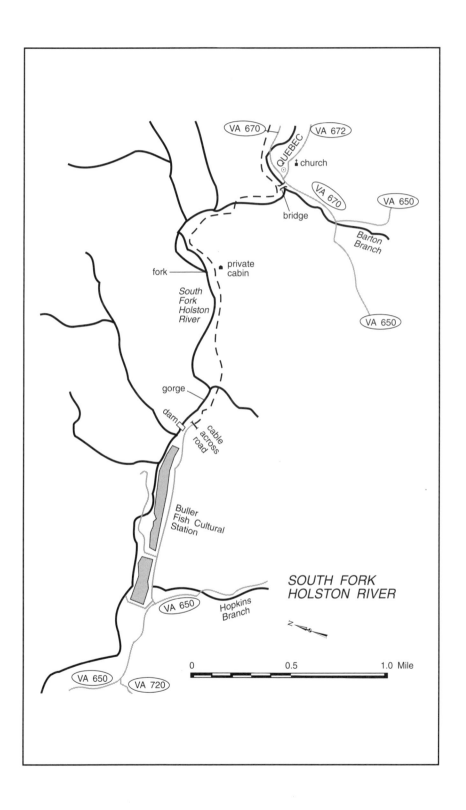

VA 670

VA 672

QUEBEC

church

VA 670

VA 650

bridge

Barton
Branch

fork

private
cabin

South
Fork
Holston
River

VA 650

gorge

dam

cable
across
road

Buller
Fish Cultural
Station

SOUTH FORK
HOLSTON RIVER

VA 650

Hopkins
Branch

N

VA 650

VA 720

0   0.5   1.0 Mile

liberally in surrounding lakes and warm-water fisheries. Getting back on your way, you drive upstream past a dam and reach a cable closing the road to vehicles. From here it's trout all the way.

From this point there are a couple of choices, one being to wade the stream above the dam from where the impoundment becomes shallow enough into a gorge with some pretty tough white water. (By the way, this is chest-wader water even during the low-water months of summer, as the Holston is well fed by mountain streams and limestone springs all along its course.) The other choice will be to shoulder your waders and hike up a fair-sized hill over a mile to where the river levels out somewhat. It's a relief to find a trout stream of this width in the Virginia Highlands, and backcasting is relatively free of snags. Before starting your uphill hike, casting from the bank into the deep water above the dam will attract some darting rainbows, but these fish have seen a dry fly before and invariably turn away at the last second.

At the upper level there are long stretches of still water over deep pockets among the rocks. Trout may be seen popping flies softly from the surface of the relatively quiet water. Occasional hatches of Green Drake, Hendrickson, Light Cahill, and stone flies occur, with the dictates of match-the-hatch determining which to tie on, because of the variety of flies found here. In the rapids a wet Olive Dun or Coachman may be preferable, with an occasional big brown going after a Wooly Bugger.

Allow a day to explore the Holston's South Fork, as each bend presents a new set of challenges—casting approaches and varied insect life—to be analyzed. At the mountaintop is a large private cabin with a fork in the river just above it. The water runs across a stream-wide slate ledge and dumps into a foaming trough of dark-green water just beneath the fork. This spot is worth an hour of fishing in itself. Above the fork there is no stocking and few native brooks and rainbows. For the hardier fisherman who still hasn't had enough of this seductive river, there's plenty of smaller water upstream. Downstream is some put-and-take water, with citation holdover browns and some big rainbows.

Directions: At exit 16 from I-81 follow VA 16 north to US 11; turn left onto US 11 and after five blocks, turn left onto VA(s) 658. Follow 658 south to a left on VA(s) 657, and after a short distance another left onto

VA(s) 650. Follow 650 to the Buller Fish Cultural Station, turning in at the sign there. Go upstream on a gravel road, past the fish hatchery, to a cable across the road barring vehicles.

Another access to the South Holston may be gained west of VA 16 near Sugar Grove, off VA(s) 672 right at the intersection of VA(s) 670, where a sign indicates Valley View Baptist Church. The first glance may be misleading, as a wooden bridge leads across the Holston into someone's front yard. The homeowner is very understanding of stream-lashers, however, and enormous rainbows can be spotted straightaway beneath the bridge. Working downstream, taking care not to damage the grass, you can often find more good-sized trout flashing bottoms-up while working nymphs and snails on the bed. Then suddenly the river is surrounded by woods, and only a dim path parallels its course. It's narrower here, resembling a true Virginia Highlands stream, and it harbors some smaller natives for a good distance downstream.

HURRICANE CREEK

STREAM TYPE: Freestone • USGS Whitetop Mountain
DeLorme 23

The Virginia Highlands is a specific region in the state's southwest panhandle wedged between Tennessee and Kentucky. Mount Rogers, the state's highest mountain, is located here, along with ridges almost equaling its height. The wealth of the area is in its waters, which roll exuberantly from the mountaintops in some locations and quietly trickle through the gorges thousands of feet below in others. The Hurricane is an example of those quiet, low-lying streams of the Highlands.

Although hundreds of feet below the brow of Seng Mountain, this little stream has an active brook trout life of its own, with small rapids and holes alternating. By the way, "seng" is the local vernacular for ginseng, whose root is renowned for medicinal and aphrodisiac qualities and which still brings income to those mountain people hardy enough to break through the underbrush where there are no paths. Occasionally during midcast you may be overrun by a wild-eyed, lean bunch of people loping through the woods. These are the seng-gatherers, usually active in early fall when the special brilliant yellow of the ginseng plant is unmistakable from hundreds of yards away. During June the woods are slashed with a similar bold color, the light yellow to deep orange of wild azalea blossoms.

Hurricane Creek, also called Hurricane Branch, is small enough to be fished without benefit of waders. Red and black ants are effective, as are olive nymphs cast up into the rapids and allowed to cascade over into holed-out rocks. Don't expect too much mayfly action, as the small, restless Hurricane is not ideal for their hatches.

Directions: From I-81 take Exit 16 south on US 16 into the Mount Rogers National Recreation Area. A worthwhile stop is the area headquarters, where a detailed map may be obtained, along with answers to any questions. Proceed south on 16 to a sign indicating a right turn onto VA(s) 650 leading to the Hurricane Campground. From here it's all downhill, with the road rimming hundred-foot drop-offs worthy of the Rockies, but with more trees to catch you. Finally you reach bottom, and cross the Hurricane on a bridge into the campground.

LAUREL CREEK

STREAM TYPE: Freestone • USGS Hutchinson's Rock • DeLorme 39

The first stream encountered on FR 222 in Tazewell County is Laurel Creek, crossed there by a wooden bridge. There is a stocking sign posted, and a well-used clearing. From the bridge upstream, Laurel Creek departs from the road up onto the side of Clinch Mountain. It becomes a native trout fishery along the way, well worth the effort of wading and climbing upstream.

Downstream there is a very rough and rutted road following Laurel Creek, eventually joining up with VA(s) 601. The downstream section is much more conveniently reached by turning east off VA 16 in the Freestone Valley, and following VA(s) 601 up the Laurel. Despite its relatively small size, this stream produces some citation-length rainbows and brooks. Its frequent rapids and falls will quickly dunk a dry fly, making streamers and Muddler Minnows more practical. Use a quick wrist on your retrieve.

Directions: This and the next two streams can be reached by the same route: leave I-81 at Exit 16 on VA 16, and go north. Follow VA 16 north past Hungry Mother State Park, and across Walker and Brushy mountains. Then just over the crest of Clinch Mountain, behind a cut bank, there's a dirt road leading down the mountain to the right. There is no marking and no route sign, but this is FR 222. Look down the mountainside for a dirt road snaking its way to the east. If you continue down Clinch Mountain on VA 16 to Thompson Valley, you've missed it, but fortunately the turnoff is much more visible as you return southbound. A stop at Monk's Store is a good idea, as the proprietor has fished the local waters for trout for many years and is willing to share his experience, as well as directions.

FR 222 is a well-traveled dirt-and-gravel roadway, with hunting cabins scattered among the Jefferson National Forest land. You will cross a wooden bridge spanning Laurel Creek, with plenty of parking space at streamside.

LICK CREEK

STREAM TYPE: Freestone • USGS Hutchinson's Rock • DeLORME 39

A successful local trout fisherman puts Lick Creek high on his list, second only to the South Holston. According to him, plenty of trout can be caught on this modest stream even in late fall, and not necessarily at painfully early morning hours. He uses small weighted blackflies tied wet and whatever terrestrials are crawling on a given day.

AUTHOR'S NOTE: Although I have had very little experience fishing this stream, one incident stands out. I was walking the bank idly scanning its waters when suddenly I realized what I was looking at was a fourteen- or fifteen-inch rainbow fanning its tail in the sunlight. Because of its size, unusual in these waters, I rushed back to my vehicle for my fly rod. Returning carefully to the hole, I followed all the correct procedures, crouching low, moving slowly, and inching to within casting distance. It was a flat area, with no natural cover, and as I raised my WondeRod for a backcast, the fish vanished. I just caught a glimpse of him streaking under the submerged roots of an oak tree, where he faded into a cave he had staked out there.

I tried everything, drifting an assortment of flies, ants, and minnow replicas before his hiding place. But no amount of tweaking, darting, drifting, or dangling would bring him out of his sulk.

Directions: Proceed as for Laurel Creek, above. Approximately 7 miles down FR 222, past Laurel Creek, you begin seeing good trout water on Lick Creek to the left of the road. Some exploring along the bank, where the stream departs from the road, reveals excellent fishing.

ROARING FORK

STREAM TYPE: Freestone • USGS Hutchinson's Rock • DELORME 39

It is suggested that you bandolier your waders and put on a good pair of hiking boots before descending the trail to Roaring Fork. As you begin the walk down to fishing waters, a barely visible sign marks the boundary of the Jefferson National Forest Wilderness Area surrounding this stream. To the right of the trail are upended flat rocks painted yellow, with mileages marked at 3.0 and 2.5. True to its designation, this is an area free of beer cans and gum wrappers, with a peace and quiet so deep it seems leftover from the last century. You may hear an occasional deer crashing away from its disturbed morning bed. Then, halfway down the mountainside, there's a faint sound from below which could be mistaken for wind in the trees, but which as you approach becomes the unmistakable sound of falling water. Aptly named, Roaring Fork deceives you into believing its roar lies just below the next line of trees, when in reality it's still half a mile down.

As the roar becomes louder, you suddenly U-turn back around a thick wall of rhododendron, and there's the stream. And what a trout stream it is! The difficulties of finding your way are all at once worth the trip—or a trip ten times greater.

The pools have the look of a Waterford crystal tinted with just a bare hint of moss green. There are in fact a few hardy strands of moss trailing from underwater boulders. The subtle touch of green to the quieter water, contrasted with the pure cut-glass of the rapids and falls, gives Roaring Fork a look of unreality, especially against its background of thirty-foot rhododendron. There are no boot prints along the bank, only some hefty-sized deer tracks. This is what Appalachian trout fishing is all about, a purely native trout stream, where it's even possible to see brookies spawning on a gravel strand. When you reach this stream, without a stocking sign in sight, it belongs to you and no one else. The only clue that other *Homo sapiens* have touched the area is a birch sapling lashed between two trees, presumably to hold a lean-to for some wilderness camper.

Small black wet flies, maybe a Number 16 Black-and-Gold or Black Demon, are recommended here. It may help to wrap just a touch of lead about the leader to keep the fly down around the dark-green chambers beneath boulders. Number 16 black and red ants are recommended later in the season, as well as a Wooly Worm quartered upstream across the current. An unusual spate of warm Indian Summer has been known to bring some hatches to Roaring Fork in late October, more than likely caddis flies. Autumn days like these in the southern Appalachians make fall and winter not only feasible for fishing but the favorite time of year for Virginia fly-fishermen, including some dry-fly purists.

Walking downstream, you will see a series of small waterfalls, tumbling into huge granite cups, with stone-and-gravel bottom, in some instances too deep for the bottom to be seen. Bordered on either side by rhododendron, the banks of Roaring Fork still afford gaps for comfortable backcasts, with timber mature enough to eliminate bramble thickets. It is a stalking stream, with plenty of boulders and cut banks as cover to overcome the trout's visibility advantage. Roaring Fork can contribute a lot of wear to the knees of your waders.

There is a downside to Roaring Fork, as it is borderline acidic, and consequently the trout population is declining. The green algae streamers are in fact a warning signal of increased acid content. This low pH is partly due to the natural ecology and partly to an inability to buffer acid rain, but regardless of cause, the stream's fishing years may be numbered.

Directions: Proceed as for Laurel Creek, above. The most interesting stretch of Roaring Fork can be reached by taking an obscure turnoff from FR 222 to the left. The only way to locate it is to mark your odometer at the intersection with VA 16, then go exactly 6.5 miles. You will cross a wooden bridge spanning Laurel Creek. Then a couple of miles along, look carefully for a "two-track" to the left, again with no marking of any kind. This little dirt road calls for a four-wheel-drive transmission, with stretches leading across rock ledges with gaps between. It leads into national forest land for exactly 2 miles, and ends abruptly at an earthworks barrier. Park here and walk down the mountain for approximately 1.25 miles. This is a good, clear trail, with no difficult stretches. Allow slightly over half an hour for the return walk.

Incidentally, farther downstream off FR 222 there is easy access to the stream, accompanied by well-trampled trails. But for the pure, undiluted Appalachian native trout experience, hiking in through the Wilderness Area is hard to top.

STRAIGHT BRANCH

STREAM TYPE: Freestone • USGS Konnarock • DeLORME 22

Straight Branch is another of the small Virginia native trout streams which require special skills. It is backed up by a dam into Beartree Lake, which is stocked with trout. Above and below the lake this is a laurel-and-rhododendron-covered fishery, with the water somewhat snuff-colored by the cedar roots surrounding it. There are stocked brook trout here, but the problem is getting a fly into the pools where they live. The interlacing network of branches arch over impoundments caused by occasional hemlock or cedar tree trunks which have been felled by nature or the Game and Inland Fisheries people.

These small pools abound with life, including several varieties of minnows and insects falling from the surrounding vegetation. It's not the sort of stream conducive to classic mayfly hatches, but rainbow trout can comfortably complete their life cycles on terrestrials and underwater life forms. There's little casting to be done, because of the near impossibility of snaking a fly between the heavy undergrowth, and consequently the Straight is not a put-and-take stream.

Below Beartree, Straight Branch widens slightly, even though it's less than six feet across in most places. The lower stretch is stocked, but it's not the sort of stream likely to attract hordes of opening-day fishermen. During midsummer the water is low, though still cool enough for good trout habitat. It's worth a trip to the Straight during the hot months just to walk into the hemlock tunnels and listen to the little stream's cool clicks and gurgles.

Directions: From I-81 take Exit 16 on VA 16 south to US 58 west. Heading west from Konnarock to Damascus on 58, take a right at the sign reading Beartree Campground. Beartree Lake is a stocked trout fishery, with prescribed swimming areas along with a sand beach.

WHITETOP LAUREL

STREAM TYPE: Freestone • USGS Konnarock • DeLorme 22

There is some confusion about the Whitetop Laurel's name. More traditional maps show a Whitetop Valley Creek and a Laurel Creek, which join at Taylor's Valley. Some of the newer maps now show a Whitetop Laurel. But when you ask any local resident about either tributary, they invariably reply, "Oh, you mean the Whitetop Laurel."

Whatever you call it, this is a premier trout stream. If you had time to fish only one trout water in the state of Virginia, it probably should be the Whitetop Laurel. It's a magnificent display of what is best among all the Virginia Highlands streams, starting with a drop from

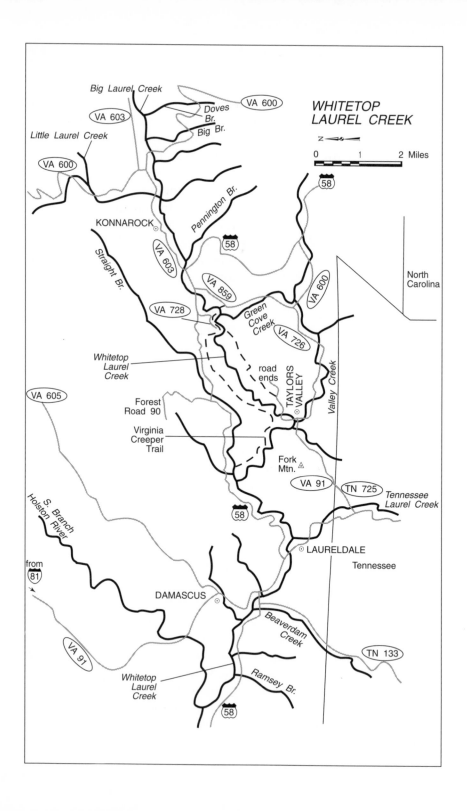

Big Laurel Creek

VA 603

Doves Br.

Big Br.

VA 600

Little Laurel Creek

VA 600

Pennington Br.

WHITETOP
LAUREL CREEK

N

0   1   2 Miles

58

KONNAROCK

VA 603

58

VA 859

VA 600

North
Carolina

Straight Br.

VA 728

Green
Cove
Creek

VA 726

Whitetop
Laurel
Creek

road
ends

TAYLORS
VALLEY

Valley Creek

VA 605

Forest
Road 90

Virginia
Creeper
Trail

Fork
Mtn. △

VA 91

TN 725

Tennessee
Laurel Creek

S. Branch
Holston River

58

from
81

LAURELDALE

Tennessee

DAMASCUS

Beaverdam
Creek

TN 133

VA 91

Whitetop
Laurel
Creek

Ramsey Br.

58

a mountaintop, through a series of cascades, to water deep enough to dive into from a ten-foot ledge without striking bottom. Finally it skirts the backyards of Damascus, where it is possible to see a suburbanite leaning on his power mower, talking to a neighbor holding a foot-and-a-half brown trout shining like a dappled ingot in the sun. Trout is a keystone in the lives of people living around the Whitetop Laurel, and everywhere there is more than a trickle, you may be sure it contains rainbows and browns, if not brookies. One Damascus citizen is reputed to trout fish 364 days of the year, missing only Christmas—and he has been known to slip out on Christmas Day if his wife turns her head.

From Damascus east to Konnarock fishing is excellent, although the real crown jewel is the Virginia Creeper Trail paralleling the stream two miles east of Damascus. Walking up the cinder trail, you'll find it is easy to imagine the pip-squeak engine which once labored up this mountain—to transport timber, since there is nothing else on the mountainside to justify the laying of the long-vanished track. From this trail, which is a delight to walk, small cleared paths lead off to the right into treasured fishing holes. The banks are moss-covered and easy to navigate, while the stream's gravelly bottom provides good boot traction.

The wooden railroad bridges are situated about twelve feet above the water, and if you can avoid casting a shadow, are perfect vantage points for observing the day's feeding habits. Plenty of hefty trout can be spotted from the bridges, along with an occasional calico sucker vacuuming up the stream floor. The bridge stanchions will invariably have a trout suspended beside them, ready to dart into the dark holes nearby at the first sign of an angler. In late May or early June you're likely to see fish feeding on a Green Drake hatch. Other good bets are Hairwing Royal Wulffs and Light Cahills.

Once the early-season pressure is off, mayfly hatches begin to hit the Whitetop Laurel, especially Light Cahill, Sulfur Dun, Green Drake, and Ginger Quill. There are lulls in the hatches, sometimes for months, due to a combination of temperatures and storm patterns. A good all-around attractor fly is an Adams Number 16, which will bring a rise even if there is no surface feeding. Toward dark, a sizable white moth will inevitably bring up fish until it's too dark to see the water. When there seems to be no possibility of rises, an Olive Caddis Pupa Number 14 works well.

The author at work on the Whitetop Laurel.

Directions: From I-81 take Exit 11 south on VA 91, which brings you into downtown Damascus, Virginia. At the intersection take US 58 east for slightly over 4 miles until you reach a sign on the right displaying the silhouette of a small steam train. Turn in here and park near the U. S. Forest Service information board. Proceed on foot up the mountain on an old cinder railroad bed which is the Virginia Creeper trail. A series of wooden "trestles," minus rails and crossties, span the Whitetop Laurel, and fishing is best above the fourth trestle, near the top of Fork Mountain.

There is another Whitetop Laurel, or so it seems, even though it's actually the same stream, and that's the one in Taylor's Valley. This stretch is reached by taking US 58 east from Damascus and turning south on VA 91. You'll cross the line and for two minutes see a bit of Johnson County, Tennessee. After a mile or so take the only paved road to the left, which is Tennessee secondary road 725, looping back into Virginia. After the pavement ends there is a temptation to turn upstream on VA(s) 726, but persevere on 725 across a wooden bridge and to the left. The road ends in what appears to be someone's front yard—and in fact it is. But you may park there and walk about a quarter of a mile upstream to a wooden trestle. From there upstream is a 3-mile stretch of regulated water, fishable only with single-hook artificial lures.

The stretch below the trestle and into Taylor's Valley is not restricted, and good fishing may be had throughout its entire length. For the hardy, fishing from US 58, up the Virginia Creeper cinder trail and across the mountain into Taylor's Valley would be more than a full day. But it would take you into some wild trout fishing which would leave material for some unbeatable winter-evening reminiscing.

ABOUT THE AUTHOR

A native Virginian, Harry Slone recalls his first encounter with angling in the state's gemlike streams. At age seven, he was hoisted onto the shoulders of an unreconstructed fly-fisher, who waded into the Blue Hole on the Bullpasture River. That senior stream-lasher then cast his Royal Coachman past the young future author, leaving an indelible memory.

An eighteen-year residence in Pennsylvania gave Slone another picture of fly-fishing, one rich in tradition and liberally documented. His return to Virginia brought him the idea of at least beginning some documentation of the Old Dominion's trout legacy. This book is the outgrowth of that comparison of Virginia with Pennsylvania.

A free-lancer in the medical field, Mr. Slone features himself as "A writer who fly-fishes rather than a fly-fishing authority who writes." He adds that all the observations in this book are the result of personal encounters with all the Virginia trout streams featured. The descriptions are therefore honest impressions of the waters and the fish they contain—maybe not what others would see but a true delineation of what he saw.

Index

Also from The Countryman Press and Backcountry Publications

The Countryman Press and its associated companies, long known for fine books on the outdoors, offer a range of practical and readable manuals for sportsmen and women.

Fish and Fishing

Fishing Small Streams with a Fly Rod, by Charles R. Meck,
  $14.95 (paper), $24.95 (deluxe cloth edition)
*Our Native Fishes: The Aquarium Hobbyist's Guide to Observing,
  Collecting and Keeping Them,* by John Quinn, $14.95
Pennsylvania Trout Streams and Their Hatches,
  by Charles R. Meck, $14.95
Taking Freshwater Game Fish, by Todd Swainbank
  and Eric Seidler, $14.95

Fly Tying

Bass Flies, by Dick Stewart, $12.95 (paper), $19.95 (cloth)
Fly Tying Tips, edited by Dick Stewart, $9.95
Universal Fly Tying Guide, by Dick Stewart, $9.95

Cookbooks

Fish and Fowl Cookery: The Outdoorsman's Home Companion,
  by Carol Vance Wary with William G. Wary, $10.95
Wild Game Cookery: The Hunter's Home Companion,
  Revised and Expanded Edition, by Carol Vance Wary, $12.95

Other books for Virginia residents and visitors:

25 Bicycle Tours on Delmarva, by John Wennersten, $9.95
25 Bicycle Tours in and around Washington, DC, by Anne Oman, $9.95
Walks and Rambles on the Delmarva Peninsula,
  by Jay Abercrombie, $9.95

We also publish guides to canoeing, hiking, walking, bicycling, and ski touring in New England, New York state, the Mid-Atlantic states, and the Midwest.

Our titles are available in bookshops and in many sporting goods stores, or they may be ordered directly from the publisher. When ordering by mail, please add $2.50 per order for shipping and handling. To order or obtain a complete catalog, please write The Countryman Press, Inc., P.O. Box 175, Woodstock, Vermont 05091.